User's Reference Guide

LCB-4491

Video connector
yellow *Red*
Sheild
black *Sheild*

A complete, detailed guide to using and enjoying your Texas Instruments TI-99/4A Computer.

Texas Instruments invented the integrated circuit, microprocessor, and microcomputer — technological milestones that made today's small computers a reality. TI is a world leader in producing reliable, affordable advanced electronics.

See important warranty information at back of book.

This book was developed by:
The Staff of the Texas Instruments Learning Center
and
The Staff of the Texas Instruments Personal
Computer Division

Artwork and layout were coordinated and executed by:
Schenck Design Associates, Inc.

Federal Communications Commission Requirements Concerning Radio Frequency Interference

The Texas Instruments TI-99/4A Computer generates and uses radio frequency (RF) energy. *If not installed and used properly* (as outlined in the instructions provided by Texas Instruments), the computer may cause interference to radio and television reception.

The computer has been type-tested and found to comply with the limits for a Class B computing device in accordance with the specifications in Sub-part J of Part 15 of FCC Rules. These rules are designed to provide reasonable protection against radio and television interference in a residential installation. However, there is no guarantee that interference will not occur in a particular installation.

If this equipment does cause interference to radio or television reception (which you can determine by turning the equipment off and on), try to correct the interference by one or more of the following measures:

- Reorient the receiving antenna (that is, the antenna for the radio or television that is "receiving" the interference).

- Change the position of the computer with respect to the radio or television equipment that is receiving interference.

- Move the computer away from the equipment that is receiving interference.

- Plug the computer into a different wall outlet so that the computer and the equipment receiving interference are on different branch circuits.

If these measures do not eliminate the interference, please consult your dealer or an experienced radio/television technician for additional suggestions. Also, the Federal Communications Commission has prepared a helpful booklet, "How to Identify and Resolve Radio-TV Interference Problems." This booklet is available from
The US Government Printing Office
Washington, D.C. 20402

Please specify Stock Number 004-000-00345-4 when ordering copies.

WARNING: This equipment has been certified to comply with the limits for a Class B computing device, persuant to Subpart J of Part 15 of FCC Rules. Only peripherals (computer input/output devices, terminals, printers, etc.) certified to comply with the Class B limits may be attached to this computer. Operation with non-certified peripherals is likely to result in interference to radio and TV reception.

ISBN#0-89512-048-8
Library of Congress Catalog #81-51829

Table of Contents

Table of Contents

Table of Contents

Table of Contents

General Information

INTRODUCTION

You are about to be introduced to the exciting new world of the personal computer. Until just a few years ago, the size, price, and complexity of computers put them beyond the reach of the individual purchaser. Today, Texas Instruments Personal Computers bring you remarkable computing power in affordable, compact units that can be easily set up in your home, office, or school.

Whether you have years of computer experience or have never worked with computers before, the innovative and flexible features of your computer offer you a wide variety of applications. Within minutes, you can begin using your computer to

- manage your personal resources
- develop projects for home and business
- bring new dimensions to education — for you and your children
- provide engaging new types of entertainment for the entire family
- and much more.

Powerful TI BASIC

TI BASIC, a simple but very powerful computer language, is built right into your Texas Instruments Computer. With TI BASIC, you can develop and use your own computer programs for applications ranging from color graphics to statistical analysis and more. This language makes your TI computer a "true" computer — not a video game or electronic toy.

Convenient Module System

The unique system of easy-to-use, snap-in *Solid State Software*™ Command Modules* assures the continued versatility and usefulness of your computer. These rugged, all solid-state modules are completely preprogrammed for you. You just snap them in, and they "prompt" you through activities, applications, games, and entertainment. With a module plugged into the computer console, you can start using your computer immediately. You can choose from a wide selection of Command Module titles. Ask your dealer to see all of them!

Tape and Diskette Programs

In addition to Command Modules, Texas Instruments offers a variety of convenient software on tape or diskette, ranging in complexity from simple games applications to high-level business and professional programs. Like Command Modules, these applications are ready for you to use, without any programming on your part. Programs on cassette tape require the Cassette Interface Cable* to connect the computer and your cassette recorder, and diskette programs require the TI Disk Memory System.* Ask you dealer to show you a list of the many tape and diskette packages available from TI and other software developers.

USING THIS BOOK

The *User's Reference Guide* is organized in the following step-by-step fashion:
- a brief discussion of the care of your new computer.
- an explanation of how to connect the computer to the monitor.
- a tour of your computer, starting with the connector outlets and including the computer keyboard.
- the accessories available for the computer.
- a BASIC reference section.

No special expertise or experience is necessary to fully enjoy and utilize your TI computer. The simple instructions we provide here and in the books enclosed with each software package, as well as the prompting you receive from the computer, are all you need to get "up and running" quickly.

PLACEMENT AND CARE

First, find the right location for your computer system. Select a place where sunlight or bright light doesn't fall directly on the screen. Also, it's best to place the system on a hard-topped non-metallic surface, such as a table. DO NOT SET THE COMPUTER CONSOLE ON TOP OF A TELEVISION SET.

Correct ventilation is necessary for the continued proper operation of your computer system. Be sure air can flow freely through all the ventilation slots on the bottoms, backs, and tops of the console and monitor (or TV set, if you're using the TI-900 Video Modulator and a TV set). Do not obstruct the ventilation or enclose the system in any way.

*sold separately

General Information

From time to time you may want to clean the surfaces of your computer. First, turn the computer OFF. Then gently wipe the surface using a damp, lint-free cloth. Do not use solvents or other cleansers to clean the computer console.

CAUTION: *Electronic equipment can be damaged by static electricity discharges.* Static electricity build-ups can be caused by walking across a carpet. If you build up a static charge and then touch the computer, a Command Module, or any accessory device, you can permanently damage the internal circuits. Always touch a metal object (a door knob, a desk lamp, etc.) before working with your computer, connecting accessory devices, or handling or inserting a Command Module. You may want to purchase a special anti-static spray for the carpeting in the room where your computer is located. This commercial preparation is usually available from local carpet, hardware, and office supply stores.

MONITOR-CONSOLE CONNECTION

When you have chosen the right location for your computer, you are ready to set up the system. The hook-up instructions to follow depend on whether you are using the TI Color Monitor or your own television set as a video display.

If You Are Using *the TI Color Monitor*

Connecting your computer to the TI Color Monitor requires only two simple steps, using the cable packed with the monitor.

1. Connect the 5-pin plug (called a "DIN" plug) to your computer console at the point shown.

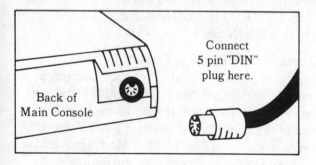

Connect 5 pin "DIN" plug here.

Back of Main Console

2. The other end of the cable (with two plugs) connects to your monitor. Connect the larger plug to the outlet labeled "VIDEO" on the back of your monitor and the smaller plug to the outlet labeled "AUDIO" on the back of your monitor as shown below.

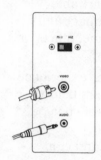

Note: Do not attach the console directly to a television set using this cable. Connection of the console to a television receiver must be made using the TI-900 Video Modulator.

If You Are Using *Your Television Set and the TI-900 Video Modulator*

CAUTION: Federal Radiation Emission Standards set forth in Regulation 21 CFR 1020 do not apply to color television receivers manufactured before January 15, 1970. To avoid possible exposure to radiation emissions in excess of the standards, Texas Instruments recommends the use of the Video Modulator only with TV receivers manufactured after that date.

Connecting the computer to your television set requires the use of the TI-900 Video Modulator. To install the modulator, follow these steps.

1. Turn the television set and the computer OFF.
2. Remove the VHF antenna cable from your television set. (If your set does not have a standard antenna hookup similar to the one shown below, please consult the Video Modulator manual for more details.)
3. Connect the television interconnect cable, marked "TV VHF" on the TI-900 Video Modulator, to the VHF antenna terminals on your television set.

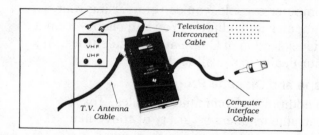

Television Interconnect Cable

VHF
UHF

T.V. Antenna Cable

Computer Interface Cable

General Information

4. Connect the VHF antenna cable that you just removed from your television set to the Video Modulator terminals, marked "ANT."
5. Remove the paper backing from the double-sided tape on the modulator and press the unit against a flat surface on your television set.
6. Connect the 5-pin "DIN" plug of the computer interface cable into the 5-pin socket on the back of the console.

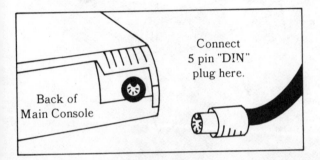

Back of Main Console

Connect 5 pin "DIN" plug here.

Once the modulator is installed, set the "CH. SELECT" switch on your Video Modulator and the channel selector on your televsion set to the same channel, either channel 3 or 4. If there is a television station operating on one of these channels in your area, set the "CH. SELECT" switch and the television to the other channel.

Then, to use your television set as a computer display, set the "TV/COMP." switch to "COMP." (When you are ready to watch television again, set the "TV/COMP." switch to "TV.")

Connect Power Cords

Next, connect the power cord (with transformer) to the computer. Connect the small 4-pin plug end into the outlet on the back of the computer as indicated below. *Notice that the pins only line up one way.*

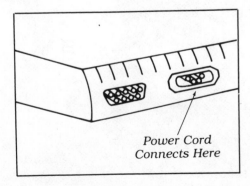

Power Cord Connects Here

Then, plug the power transformer into a regular wall outlet. It is best to plug the transformer into a wall outlet that is continuously "live," not one controlled by a wall switch. You may want to secure the power transformer to the wall outlet as in the sketch above. (*Note:* Some wall plates may not have a screw location that matches the transformer.)

Finally, plug either the monitor or television power cord into a continuously "live" wall outlet. (The color monitor is designed to operate on 120 volt 60 Hz AC. DO NOT ATTEMPT TO OPERATE THE UNIT ON DC.) The power supply cord has a plug with two blades and one grounding pin as a safety feature. DO NOT ATTEMPT TO PLUG THE POWER CORD INTO A 2-HOLE WALL OUTLET. If the plug does not fit your wall outlet, contact an electrician.

Check the Connections

Before you turn on your computer, follow these steps:
- Check to see that all connections are secure.
- Make sure both the computer and the monitor or your television set are plugged into a live wall outlet.
- If you are using your own television set and a TI-900 Video Modulator, set the "TV/COMP." switch on the modulator to "COMP." and be sure that the "CH. SELECT" switch on the modulator and the channel selector on your television are set to the same channel (either 3 or 4, whichever is not a broadcasting channel in your area).

General Information

A TOUR OF YOUR COMPUTER

Your computer console is the central part of your computer system. It's designed so that all of the other units of the system easily connect to this console. No tools are required.

Getting Started

Let's look at the front and right side of your computer.

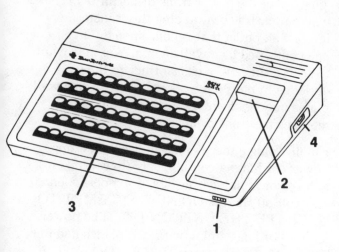

1 This is the ON/OFF switch. The small light next to the switch indicates when the computer is ON.

2 Command Module software* snaps into this outlet.

3 This keyboard is used to type information into the computer.

4 This outlet is for optional peripheral accessories. Details are included with the appropriate peripheral.

This is the back and left side of the console:

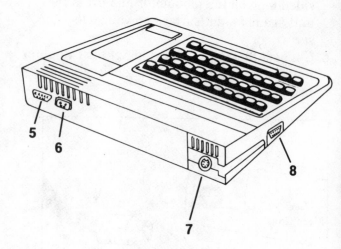

5 The Cassette Interface Cable* connects to the console at this 9-pin "D" outlet.

6 The Power Cord attaches to the console at this 4-pin outlet.

7 This 5-pin connector (also called a DIN connector) is for audio-out and video-out. This connector will insert easily when properly aligned.

8 The Wired Remote Controllers connect to this 9-pin outlet. Details are included with the accessory.

(*Note:* Do not confuse this 9-pin outlet with the 9-pin outlet on the back of the console. They are not interchangeable.)

*sold separately

General Information

A Tour of the Keyboard
Let's take a close look at the keyboard.

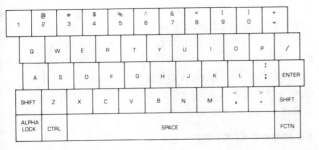

The keyboard is like a standard typewriter, with keys of several types. Pressing any key causes its *lower-case* (small capital) character to display on the screen, and holding down the **SHIFT** key while pressing any other key returns the *upper-case* (large capital) character for that key. Except for the alphabetical keys, each key's upper-case character is printed at the top of the key face, while the lower-case character is printed at the bottom.

Some of the keys also have special functions, as explained in the following sections.

AUTOMATIC REPEAT
TI BASIC is designed with an automatic repeat function. If you hold down the **SPACE BAR** or any character key for more than one second, that character is repeated until you release the key.

ALPHABET KEYS
All alphabetical symbols are typed into the computer using the alphabet keys. To capitalize letters, hold down the **SHIFT** key and press the letter key, just as you would on a standard typewriter keyboard.

ALPHA LOCK
Pressing **ALPHA LOCK** locks all the alphabetical keys into their upper-case mode. The number and punctuation keys are not affected. When you press **ALPHA LOCK** again, the keyboard returns to normal operation.

Note: When you are using the Wired Remote Controllers, **ALPHA LOCK** must be in the off (up) position.

NUMBER KEYS
The number keys are located on the top row of your computer keyboard. If you have previous typing experience, you need to be aware of two differences between this keyboard and some typewriter keyboards. With the computer, you cannot type the letter "L" as the number "1." Also, never substitute the letter "O" for a zero. The computer screen displays the letter "O" with squared corners and displays a zero with rounded corners, so you'll be able to distinguish them.

PUNCTUATION AND SYMBOL KEYS
The computer keyboard has the punctuation and symbol keys which appear on a standard typewriter, as well as several others used in computer applications. To type any symbol which appears on the bottom of a key face, simply press the key. To type the upper symbol, hold down the **SHIFT** key and press the symbol key. Notice that punctuation marks and symbols also appear on the fronts of some keys. To type these symbols, hold down the **FCTN** key and press the key.

SPECIAL FUNCTION KEYS
Several keys have varying functions in TI BASIC, some Command Module software, and other applications. The use of the keys is described in detail in the appropriate sections of this *Guide* or in the manuals that accompany the various modules.

To activate any special function, except **ENTER**, hold down the **FCTN** key and press the letter or number key.

FCTN = (QUIT)
Pressing **QUIT** (at any time) returns the computer to the master title screen. *Note:* When you press **QUIT**, all data or program material you have entered will be erased.

ENTER
In most cases, pressing the **ENTER** key tells the computer to accept the information you have just finished typing. Additional functions will be explained in the appropriate manuals.

General Information

FCTN ← (LEFT)

Pressing the *left-arrow* key (backspace) moves the cursor to the left. The cursor does not erase or change the characters on the screen as it passes over them.

FCTN → (RIGHT)

Pressing the *right-arrow* key (forwardspace) moves the cursor to the right. As the cursor passes over the characters printed on the screen, it does not alter them in any way.

FCTN ↑ (UP)
FCTN ↓ (DOWN)

These keys have various functions according to the specific application where they are used. See the TI BASIC section in this book and the appropriate software manuals for a complete explanation of their use.

FCTN 1 (DEL)

The **DEL**ete key is used to delete a letter, number, or other character from the lines you type.

FCTN 2 (INS)

The **INS**ert key is used to insert a letter, number, or other character into the lines you type.

FCTN 3 (ERASE)

Pressing the **ERASE** key before pressing **ENTER** erases the line you are presently typing.

FCTN 4 (CLEAR)

This key is normally used to clear from the screen any information you have typed (before pressing **ENTER**). It also has additional functions in TI BASIC. See "Special Keys" in the BASIC Reference Section of this book for details of its use in TI BASIC.

Other keys have special functions in software applications. Some of these are:

FCTN 5 (BEGIN)
FCTN 6 (PROC'D)
FCTN 7 (AID)
FCTN 8 (REDO)
FCTN 9 (BACK)

SPECIAL CONTROL KEYS

The TI computer also has control characters which are used primarily for telecommunications. For a list of the standard ASCII control characters included in your computer, see "Control Key Codes" in the *Appendix*. To enter a control character, hold down the **CTRL** key and press the appropriate letter or number key.

Keyboard Overlay

A two-level strip overlay is included with your computer. You can use this overlay to help you more easily identify certain keys that are used in combination with the **FCTN** and **CTRL** keys.

The top level of functions, identified by the red dot, are called control keys. To access these keys, hold down the **CTRL** key, marked with a red dot, while pressing the appropriate number or alphabet key. The second level of functions, identified by the light gray dot, are accessed by holding down the **FCTN** key, also marked with a light gray dot, while pressing the appropriate number or letter key.

MATH OR OPERATION KEYS

The Math keys (or operation keys) are the keys used to instruct the computer to add, subtract, multiply, divide, and raise a number to a power.

The symbols for addition, subtraction, and equals are the usual ones you're familiar with, but the multiplication and division symbols may be new to you.

+ Addition
− Subtraction
* Multiplication
/ Division
= Equals

The "caret" key (∧) is also used for mathematical operations:

SHIFT ∧

This symbol tells the computer to perform exponentiation (raising a number to a power). Since 5^3 cannot be easily printed on your screen, the computer interprets 5 ∧ 3 to mean that three is an exponent.

General Information

The following keys are used to indicate mathematical relationships in TI BASIC:

SHIFT >   "Greater than"; this symbol is used to compare two quantities.

SHIFT <   "Less than"; this symbol is also used to compare two quantities.

SPACE BAR

The **SPACE BAR** is the long bar at the bottom of the keyboard. It operates just like the space bar on a regular typewriter. When you press the **SPACE BAR**, the computer leaves a blank space between words, letters or numbers.

The **SPACE BAR** can also be used to erase characters already on the screen. (See the section titled "Correcting Errors.")

Correcting Errors

To correct a typing error before you press **ENTER,** move the cursor back to the character you want to change (using the *left-arrow* key). Retype the correct character (or characters); then move the cursor back to the end of the word or phrase you were typing (using the *right-arrow* key).

You can erase errors by using the **SPACE BAR.** Backspace (using the *left-arrow* key) to a point where you want to begin erasing. Then press the **SPACE BAR** to move the cursor over the characters on the screen. The characters are erased.

In certain applications, you can also make corrections using the **DEL**ete key and the **INS**ert key.

ACCESSORIES

A wide variety of accessories is available for use with the computer. These accessories expand the capabilities of your basic unit, letting you build your system as you need it.

TI Disk Memory System*

The TI Disk Memory System is a mass storage system, consisting of a TI Disk Drive Controller and one to three Disk Memory Drives. With the system, you can save your computer programs for use at a later time, as well as enjoy preprogrammed applications available on diskette. In addition, some of the Command Modules are designed to let you store data and results from your computations.

The Disk Manager Command Module is packaged with each Disk Drive Controller. With the module, you can catalog a diskette, name diskettes or files, delete files, copy diskettes or files, protect your files, and test the operation of your disk system.

TI *Solid State Speech*™ Synthesizer*

The *Solid State Speech*™ Synthesizer gives your TI computer a voice of its own and adds new excitement and enjoyment to computer applications through spoken words, phrases, and sentences. To activate the Speech Synthesizer, you must also have a specialized Command Module* plugged into your computer console. You can use the Speech Editor Command Module, the Terminal Emulator II Command Module, or any other module which is programmed for speech.

*sold separately

General Information

TI Solid State Thermal Printer*

When the TI Solid State Thermal Printer is connected to your computer, you can obtain a printed copy of your program and data to aid you in revising long programs or maintaining files of programs and results. In addition, the Thermal Printer can be used with some software applications to print screen displays or generate printed lists and reports.

The printer prints up to 32 characters on a line and prints either characters from its resident character set or special characters that you define. Special features included in the printer also let you control the amount of paper that is ejected and the spacing between lines.

TI Wired Remote Controllers*

The lightweight, compact Wired Remote Controllers add greater freedom and versatility to games, graphics, and sound applications on your computer, without the need for keyboard interaction. You can use the Remote Controllers with certain software applications or with your own TI BASIC programs.

Note: When you are using the Wired Remote Controllers, **ALPHA LOCK** must be in the off (up) position.

TI RS232 Interface*

The Texas Instruments RS232 Interface allows you to connect a wide range of EIA RS232C-compatible accessory devices to your computer. With the RS232 Interface attached to your computer, you can list programs on a printer, utilize a modem for telecommunications, print graphs on a plotter, and much more.

TI Telephone Coupler (Modem)*

Added to the RS232 Interface, the Telephone Coupler (Modem) enables your computer to communicate over telephone lines with another similarly equipped computer. If you also have a TI Command Module* designed for telecommunications, you can access subscription data base services.

TI Audio Adapter*

The Audio Adapter provides a handy connector for use with ¼"-plug headphones.

TI Memory Expansion Unit*

The Memory Expansion unit adds 32K bytes of Random Access Memory to the computer's built-in memory. In addition, the unit increases the number of accessories which can be connected to the computer. (*Note:* The Memory Expansion unit requires the use of a Command Module or an accessory designed to utilize the unit. The TI BASIC programming language built into the computer *cannot* make use of the Memory Expansion unit.)

Cassette Interface Cable

You can further expand your computer system by using audio cassette tape recorders. TI BASIC allows you to store and retrieve data you enter in the computer (programs, numerical data, etc.). By recording data on a tape, you can *save* it as a permanent record. Later you can *load* the data from the cassette tape into the computer's memory if you want to use that information again. Several of the command modules also use this feature to save and load data you've used in the module.

You can use either one or two recorders for this purpose. Using two cassette recorders is especially helpful for advanced programming applications.

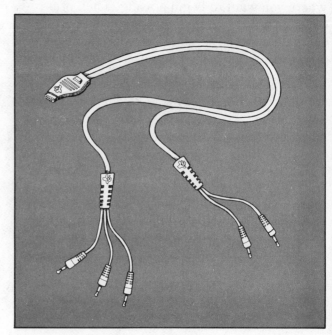

*sold separately

General Information

Many standard cassette recorders can be used with the computer. For best operation, however, they should have such features as:

- Volume control
- Tone control
- Microphone jack
- Remote jack
- Earphone or external speaker jack
- Digital tape counter (This will enable you to easily locate the correct tape position in case you want to store more than one program or data set on the same tape.)

Since motor control design varies from manufacturer to manufacturer, we have tested several different cassette recorders to determine whether they can be used with the computer. A list of recorders that appear to work well with this computer is included separately. We've also indicated the volume setting and tone control setting for each unit that give the best operating results.

Texas Instruments can assume no responsibility for any design changes made by the cassette recorder manufacturers that might affect the use of a specific recorder with the TI computer.

Carefully follow the directions for setting up and using your recorder, as described in the remainder of this section. If your cassette recorder does not appear to be compatible with the computer, try disconnecting the black wire from the remote jack on the recorder and operating the recorder manually. If you can save or load data while operating the recorder manually, but cannot do so when the black wire is connected, you may continue to operate the recorder manually or change to one of the recommended cassette units.

Note: The cassette interface cable uses the triple-plug end for cassette number 1 "CS1," and the double-plug end for cassette number 2 "CS2." Cassette unit 1 may be used for both recording (writing) and reading; cassette unit 2 may be used for writing only.

CONNECTING THE RECORDER

To connect your cassette player(s) to the computer, use the cassette interface cable, and follow these simple steps:

1. Insert the single plug end of the cable with the 9-pin "D" connector into the 9-pin outlet on the back of the console (labeled "A").

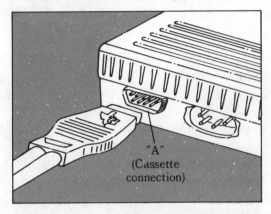

"A"
(Cassette connection)

2. Attach the triple plug ends into the cassette recorder(s) as follows:

- Insert the plug with the red wire into the microphone jack
- Insert the plug with the black wire into the remote jack (note that this plug is smaller than the other two plugs)
- Insert the plug with the white wire into the earphone jack (or external speaker jack) — CS1 only.

3. Make sure you notice how the cassettes are connected when you select either CS1 or CS2 when saving data. When loading data, only CS1 can be used. See TO SAVE/LOAD DATA section for more information.

(*Note:* You will usually elect to connect only one cassette recorder. The other plug end will simply be inactive when only one recorder is used with the computer.)

General Information

After all cables are connected, turn the tone control on your cassette player to full TREBLE or to the point indicated on the table on the separate cassette sheet. Set the volume at about half scale (if the volume control has ten positions, set it at five or at the position indicated in the table). If your cassette player does not have a tone control, you may have to set the volume control higher for best results.

Note: The Memory Expansion unit adds 32K bytes of Random Access Memory (RAM) to the built-in memory of the computer. However, even with the Memory Expansion unit available, the largest program that can be stored on a cassette tape is 12K bytes in size. Note that, although the length of the actual program is limited by the amount of available built-in memory, utilizing the Memory Expansion unit provides other advantages. For example, with the unit attached and turned on, your program can be up to 12K bytes in length, while any data generated by the program can be stored in the Memory Expansion unit. Without the unit, the program must be shorter so that both it and the generated data can be stored in the computer's built-in memory.

TO SAVE/LOAD DATA

If you have your cassette machine(s) connected to the console as instructed, you are ready to save/load data.

Before you attempt to save/load your data, make sure that:
- You are using *high quality* audio tape. Poor quality tape yields poor performance.
- The tape is *not longer* than C-60. Longer tapes are thinner and provide less fidelity.
- The cassette machine is not located within two feet of the monitor or a television set to minimize magnetic field interference.
- The tape is never placed within two feet of the monitor, a television set, an electric motor, or any other strong source of magnetic fields to avoid accidental erasure of your data.
- The system (computer console, cassette machine, and Color Monitor) is not located on a continuous metallic surface to minimize conducted noise.

- You are using only CS1 for LOAD. CS1 or CS2 can be used for SAVE.

To Save/Load Data in TI BASIC

For complete instructions on how to save and load data when you are programming in TI BASIC, see the section on the SAVE command.

To Save Data When Using a Module

After you have entered your data into the computer and connected the recorder to the computer (with a good quality tape cassette in place), you are ready to begin recording. Select the "SAVE" option offered by the module you're using. The computer then offers you a list of options for saving data. (*Note:* You'll get an error message if you select an option for a device that isn't connected to the console and turned ON.) Suppose, for example, that you want to save your data on a cassette recorder that's attached to the triple-plug end of the cassette interface cable. Select CS1 (cassette unit 1) from the options list.

From this point on, the computer guides you through the SAVE routine with on-screen instructions. (Note that the same instructions appear whether you select CS1 or CS2.) The computer controls the recorder motor power, so the tape does not start to move until you press **ENTER** at the points indicated.

Screen Instructions

* REWIND CASSETTE TAPE CS1
  THEN PRESS ENTER

Procedure

Rewind the tape *before* you press **ENTER**. If your recorder *does not* have a tape-position counter, rewind the tape all the way to the beginning. If your recorder *does* have a position counter, position the tape at the spot where you want to begin recording, and press the "stop" button on the recorder. (Write down the position for later reference.) Then press **ENTER** to continue.

General Information

* PRESS CASSETTE RECORD CS1
  THEN PRESS ENTER

Press the "record" button on the recorder, and then press **ENTER** on the computer. As soon as you do, your data will begin recording on the tape, and the screen will show this message:

* RECORDING

You may hear the sound of the encoded information as it is being stored or read from the tape unit. Several seconds of blank tape will be recorded to allow for the leader on the tape.

* PRESS CASSETTE STOP CS1
  THEN PRESS ENTER

When all the data has been recorded, press the "stop" button on the recorder, and then press the computer's **ENTER** key.

Once you've done this, you'll be asked:

* CHECK TAPE (Y OR N)?

Note: The single-letter responses (**Y, N, R,** etc.) you give when saving or loading data on a cassette tape must be upper-case characters. Hold down the **SHIFT** key, and press the appropriate letter key.

At this point you may choose to let the computer check your tape to make sure everything was recorded properly. We strongly recommend that you do so to ensure the accuracy of your tape for future use. *Note:* CS1 only.

If you decide not to check the tape, press N for no. Remove your tape, and label it for later reference.

If you want to check the tape, press Y for yes. Again, the computer guides you with the following messages:

* REWIND CASSETTE TAPE CS1
  THEN PRESS ENTER

Rewind the tape (*before* pressing **ENTER**) to the point where you began recording your data. If you stored your data at the beginning of the tape, simply rewind the tape to the beginning. If, however, you began at a point other than the beginning of the tape, rewind the tape to that position, and press the "stop" button on the recorder. Then press **ENTER**.

* PRESS CASSETTE PLAY CS1
  THEN PRESS ENTER

Press the "play" button on the recorder, and then press **ENTER**. The computer will compare the data in its memory to the data on the tape. While your tape is being checked by the computer, you'll see this message:

* CHECKING

If there are no errors, the following messages are displayed on the screen:

* DATA OK
  PRESS CASSETTE STOP CS1
  THEN PRESS ENTER

You can now remove your data tape and label it for future use.

If, however, the data were not recorded properly, you'll receive one of two error messages:

Error Message

* ERROR – NO DATA FOUND

Meaning

Your data was not recorded, or it did not play back.

PRESS R TO RECORD CS1
PRESS C TO CHECK
PRESS E TO EXIT

Error Message

* ERROR IN DATA DETECTED

Meaning

Some part of your data did not record properly.

PRESS R TO RECORD CS1
PRESS C TO CHECK
PRESS E TO EXIT

Before you go further, you may want to recheck these items:

■ Is the recorder at a proper distance from your television set (two feet or more)? ■ Is the recorder attached properly to the computer? ■ Is the cassette tape in good condition? (If in doubt, try another tape.) ■ Are the cassette recorder volume and tone adjusted correctly? Was the volume too high or too low? ■ Does the cassette tape head need cleaning? ■ Is the system located on a metal surface?

General Information

When you have checked these, you can choose one of these three options:

- Press **R** to record your data again, using the same instructions for RECORD that are discussed above.
- Press **C** to instruct the computer to check your data again.
- Press **E** to "exit" and the following message appears:

* PRESS CASSETTE STOP CS1
THEN PRESS ENTER

The "exit" key takes you back to the beginning of the "Save" option of the module. Thus, when you press **ENTER**, you see the "Save Data" screen and can try to store your data again. Just follow the instructions as they appear on the screen.

To Load Data When Using a Module

The next time you want to use the information stored on the tape, you'll need to "load" your data — that is, read the data you saved on tape *into* the memory system of the computer.* First, connect your cassette recorder(s) to your computer. Then insert into the computer the module from which you saved the information. When you're ready to "load," select the "LOAD DATA" option of the module. When the computer asks, press the **1** key to indicate the information is being read from a cassette. Then press the **1** key again to select cassette unit CS1. Remember CS1 is used for loading data.

From this point, the computer prints instructions on the screen for you to follow.

Screen Instructions

* REWIND CASSETTE TAPE CS1
THEN PRESS ENTER

Procedures

Rewind the tape *before* you press **ENTER**. Position your tape at the point from which you want to read the data into the computer (at the beginning if your recorder does not have a position counter). Then press **ENTER**.

**Due to differences in tape cassette design, a tape recorded by one model of recorder may not be readable by another model of recorder.*

Screen Instructions

* PRESS CASSETTE PLAY CS1
THEN PRESS ENTER

Procedures

Press the "play" button on the recorder and the **ENTER** key on the computer. The information is read from the tape and entered into the computer's memory. While the computer is reading the tape, the following message appears on the screen:

* READING

It takes some time to read in the data, depending on the amount of information stored. When the computer finishes reading the data, it tells you whether or not it read the data properly. If the data was read correctly, you'll see the following messages on the screen:

* DATA OK
* PRESS CASSETTE STOP CS1
THEN PRESS ENTER

You're now ready to begin working with the module.

If, however, the data has not been entered properly into the computer's memory, you'll see one of several "error" messages. Follow the directions on the screen to try to load your data again.

If you still have difficulty, you'll want to make sure:

- you are loading the correct tape
- the tape is positioned at the correct starting place for the data you are loading
- the tape has not been damaged or accidentally erased
- the recorder is a proper distance from your television set (two feet or more)
- the recorder is attached properly to the computer
- the cassette recorder volume is adjusted correctly
- the system is not located on a metal surface
- the tape was recorded with your cassette unit or an identical model
- the cassette tape head is clean
- you are using cassette unit 1

BASIC
Reference
Section

BASIC Reference Section

Introduction

This section of your *User's Reference Guide* provides a complete explanation of all of the commands and statements that are a part of the TI BASIC language built right into your computer. As mentioned earlier, BASIC is a computer language designed to be easy for beginners to use, yet powerful enough to allow you to use your computer for a whole host of applications. There are three different paths available to help you learn TI BASIC.

If you're a beginner — and have never had any experience with programming — the best place to begin is with the *Beginner's BASIC* book included with your computer. The book is intended to be an enjoyable, quick, self-paced first experience with programming in TI BASIC. Once you've become familiar with BASIC, this reference guide will provide the in-depth, ready reference to terms and information you'll want at your fingertips as you enjoy the experience of programming.

If you've had some programming experience — and just want to get familiar with TI BASIC and how it works on your computer — we've provided a series of applications programs at the end of this manual. These programs start out at a very simple level and progressively become more complex. Exploring these programs will illustrate for you the use of many of the statements in TI BASIC. This reference manual provides in-depth information when you need it.

For those of you with some programming experience who may not have programmed in BASIC or who want to "brush up" as you begin using your computer, we recommend that you begin with Herbert Peckham's excellent book, *Programming BASIC with the TI Home Computer,* which provides a rapid, higher-level learning experience in BASIC. It is available at most popular bookstores.

For the knowledgeable — once you've gained proficiency in programming — this guide will serve as your primary reference on TI BASIC statements and commands, providing those details that need refreshing from time to time. TI BASIC conforms to the American National Standard for Minimal BASIC. Additional features in TI BASIC, such as color graphics, sound, and many others, are also described in this manual. If you are an experienced BASIC programmer, you should have little trouble jumping right into TI BASIC and using it.

BASIC Reference Section

How This Section Is Organized

This reference guide is organized with usability as the key goal, and is divided into the following functional groups.

1. General Information
2. Commands
3. General Program Statements
4. Input-Output Statements
5. Color Graphics and Sound
6. Built-In Numeric Functions
7. Built-In String Functions
8. User-Defined Functions
9. Arrays
10. Subroutines
11. File Processing

A glossary of often-used terms is found in the back of this manual.

Notational Conventions

At the beginning of the discussion for each TI BASIC command or statement, a line appears which shows the general format for entering the command or statement. Certain notational conventions have been used in these format lines. These conventions are discussed here to help you understand how they are used.

{ } — The braces indicate that you have a choice of what to use. You may use only one of the items given within the braces.

[ ] — The brackets indicate that the item within is optional. You may use it if you wish, but it is not required.

. . . — The ellipsis indicates that the preceding item may be repeated as many times as you desire.

italics — Words appearing in italics are a general description of the item or items that need to appear there. When words are printed in italics, you need to enter your own choice in place of the italicized words when you enter the statement or command.

Examples

For each statement or command in this manual, program examples are shown at the right. Each line you must enter is indicated by the prompt character (>) to the left of the line, just as it appears on the screen. Lines which the computer places on the screen do not show the prompt character.

The examples shown in this book are printed in upper-case (large capital) letters. If you want to reproduce the examples exactly as you see them here, press down the **ALPHA LOCK** key. In most cases the computer accepts either upper-case or lower-case letters. However, when you LIST a program, the screen displays all reserved words, variable names, and subprogram names as large capitals.

General Information

Introduction

Once your computer is set up, it is a simple process to begin using TI BASIC. When you turn on your computer, the master computer title screen appears. Press any key on the keyboard to get the master selection list to be displayed. When the master selection list appears, press the **1** key to select TI BASIC. The screen is now blank except for the words "TI BASIC READY" and a prompt character (>) followed by a flashing cursor (■). Whenever the cursor is on the screen, the computer is waiting for you to enter something. The prompt character marks the beginning of each line you type.

Each line of the screen can display up to 28 characters. Each statement or command may be up to four screen lines in length. When you have completely filled one screen line, the cursor automatically moves down to the next line as you continue typing. When you have completely filled four lines, the computer will accept more characters, but the cursor will remain in the same position. Each character you enter will replace the last character of the line.

All of the keys discussed in the Special Keys section may be used in editing program lines before you press the **ENTER** key. To change anything in a program line after you have pressed **ENTER**, you can retype the entire program line making the desired corrections as you type in the line again or you can enter Edit Mode. Note that whenever you do any editing on a program, all open files are closed (see OPEN statement), and all variables become undefined.

The remainder of this section gives information which applies to many commands and statements in TI BASIC.

```
 TI BASIC READY
>■
```

```
>NEW

>10 A=2
>RUN

 ** DONE **

>PRINT A
  2

>20 B=3
>PRINT A
  0
```

Special Keys

Several keys have special functions in TI BASIC. These keys are discussed here.

ENTER — When you press the **ENTER** key, the computer accepts the program line you have just finished typing. Remember that you may use up to four screen lines for each program line before you press **ENTER**.

FCTN = (QUIT) — When you press **QUIT**, the computer leaves TI BASIC and returns to the master computer title screen. When the computer leaves TI BASIC, the program and all data stored in memory is erased. Note that this key does not close open files (see OPEN statement). Thus, it is preferable to use the BYE command to leave BASIC.

FCTN ↑ (UP) — The Up-Arrow key works exactly like the **ENTER** key, except in Edit Mode.

FCTN ↓ (DOWN) — The Down-Arrow key works exactly like the **ENTER** key, except in Edit Mode.

FCTN ← (LEFT) — The Left-Arrow (backspace) key moves the cursor one position to the left every time it is pressed. When the cursor moves over a character it does not delete or change it in any way. If the cursor reaches the beginning of the line, pressing the Left-Arrow key has no effect.

FCTN → (RIGHT) — The Right-Arrow (forwardspace) key moves the cursor one position to the right each time it is pressed. Using this key allows you to move the cursor over a character without deleting or changing it in any way. If the cursor reaches the end of the line (4 screen lines), pressing the Right-Arrow key has no effect.

FCTN 2 (INS) — The Insert key is used to insert characters in the middle of a program line. To insert characters, position the cursor (using **FCTN ←** or **FCTN →**) over the character immediately to the right of the place where you wish to insert characters, then press the Insert key. After you have pressed the Insert key, each time you press a character, the cursor and every character of the program line that is not to the left of the cursor is moved one position to the right. The character corresponding to the key you pressed is then inserted in the blank position left by the shifting of the cursor and other characters. Note that characters shifted off the end of the program line are deleted from the line. When you have finished inserting characters, press any other special key listed above, except **QUIT**.

Special Keys

FCTN 1 (DEL) — The Delete key is used to delete characters from the program line. To delete characters, position the cursor (using **FCTN ←** or **FCTN →**) over the character you wish to delete, then press the Delete key. When you press the Delete key, the character under the cursor is deleted and all characters of the program line to the right of the cursor are moved one position to the left. The cursor does not move. A blank space is used to fill the position at the right end of the program line left by the shifting of the characters.

FCTN 4 (CLEAR) — The Clear or Break key has *two* functions, depending on when you use it.

■ When this key is pressed while a program is running, a breakpoint will be taken at the next program line to be executed. This key allows you to temporarily stop a program while it is running. Note that you must continue to hold the Break key until the program stops running. When you stop running a program using the Break key, the message "BREAKPOINT AT line-number" is displayed. The program line designated by the line-number has not been performed. You can start the program running again where you stopped by entering the CONTINUE command.

■ When the Clear key is pressed while typing in a program line, the line scrolls up on the screen and is not entered. This key has additional functions in Edit Mode and in Number Mode.

FCTN 3 (ERASE) — The Erase key erases the entire program line which you are typing. The line is not entered. This key works differently in Edit Mode and Number Mode.

SPACE BAR The Space Bar moves the cursor one position to the right each time it is pressed. If you move the cursor over a character using the Space Bar, that character is replaced by the space character.

Blank Spaces

In general, a blank space can occur almost anywhere in a program without affecting the execution of the program. However, any extra blank spaces you put in that are not required will be deleted when the program line is displayed by the EDIT, NUM, or LIST command. There are some places where blank spaces must not appear, specifically:

(1) within a line number
(2) within a reserved word
(3) within a numeric constant
(4) within a variable name

The following are some examples of incorrect use of blank spaces. The correct line appears in the column at the right.

(1) 1 00 PRINT "HELLO"
(2) 110 PR INT "HOW ARE YOU?"
(3) 120 LET A = 1 00
(4) 130 LET CO ST = 24.95

Examples:

```
>100 PRINT "HELLO"
>110 PRINT "HOW ARE YOU?"
>120 LET A=100
>130 LET COST=24.95
```

All reserved words in a program should be immediately preceded and followed by one of the following:

- a blank space
- an arithmetic operator (+ − */ ∧)
- the string operator (&)
- a special character used in a particular statement format (< = >(),;:#)
- end of line (**ENTER** key)

Line Numbers

Each program is comprised of a sequence of BASIC language program lines ordered by line number. The line number serves as a label for the program line. Each line in the program begins with a line number which must be an integer between 1 and 32767, inclusive. Leading zeroes may be used but are ignored by the computer. For example: 033 and 33 will be read as 33. You need not enter lines in sequential order; they will be automatically placed that way by the computer.

When you run the program, the program lines are performed in ascending sequential order until:
(1) a branch instruction is performed (see "General Program Statements")
(2) an error occurs which causes the program to stop running (see "Error Messages")
(3) the user interrupts the running of the program with a BREAK command or by using the Break key **(CLEAR)**
(4) a STOP statement or END statement is performed
(5) the statement with the largest line number is performed

If you enter a program line with a line number less than 1 or greater than 32767, the message "BAD LINE NUMBER" will be displayed and the line will not be entered into memory.

Examples:

```
>NEW

>100 A=27.9
>110 B=31.8
>120 PRINT A;B
>130 END


>RUN
  27.9  31.8

 ** DONE **
```

```
>0 A=2

 * BAD LINE NUMBER

>33000 C=4

 * BAD LINE NUMBER
```

Numeric Constants

Numeric constants must be either positive or negative real numbers. You may enter numeric constants with any number of digits. Values are maintained internally in seven radix-100 digits. This means that numbers will have 13 or 14 decimal digits depending on the value of the number.

Scientific Notation

Very large or very small numbers are easily handled using scientific notation. A number in scientific notation is expressed as a base number (mantissa) times ten raised to some power (exponent).

$$\text{Number} = \text{Mantissa} \times 10^{\text{Exponent}}$$

To enter a number using scientific notation:

First, enter the mantissa (be sure to enter a minus sign first if it's negative).

Enter the letter "E" (must be an upper-case E).

Enter the power of 10 (if it is negative, enter the minus sign before you enter the exponent).

The following are some examples of how numbers in scientific notation are entered.

Number	Entered as
3.264×10^4	3.264E4
-98.77×10^{21}	$-98.77E21$ or $-9.877E22$
5.691×10^{-5}	$5.691E-5$
-2.47×10^{-17}	$-2.47E-17$

Numeric constants are defined in the range of $-9.9999999999999E127$ to $-1E-128$, 0, and $1E-128$ to $9.9999999999999E127$.

Underflow — If an entered or computed number, when rounded, is greater than $-1E-128$ and less than $1E-128$, then an underflow occurs. When an underflow occurs, the computer replaces the value of the number with a zero and the program continues running. No warning or error is given.

Overflow — If a number is entered or computed whose value when rounded is greater than $9.9999999999999E127$ or less than $-9.9999999999999E127$, an overflow occurs. When an overflow occurs, the constant is replaced by the computer's limit, a warning is given with the message "NUMBER TOO BIG," and the program continues running. The computer's limit is $-9.9999999999999E127$ or $9.9999999999999E127$ as appropriate. Note that "**" is printed if the exponent is greater than 99.

Examples:

```
>PRINT 1.2
 1.2

>PRINT -3
 -3

>PRINT 0
 0
```

```
>PRINT 3.264E4
 32640

>PRINT -98.77E21
 -9.877E+22
```

```
>PRINT 0
 0
```

```
>PRINT -9E-130
 0

>PRINT 9E-142
 0
```

```
>PRINT 97E136

 * WARNING:
   NUMBER TOO BIG
 9.99999E+**

>PRINT -108E144

 * WARNING:
   NUMBER TOO BIG
 -9.99999E+**
```

String Constants

A string constant is a string of characters (including letters, numbers, spaces, symbols, etc.) enclosed in quotes. Spaces within string constants are not ignored and are counted as characters in the string. All characters on the keyboard that can be displayed may be used in a string constant. A string constant is limited by the length of the input line (112 characters or four lines on the screen).

When a PRINT or DISPLAY statement is performed, the surrounding quote marks are not displayed. If you wish to have words or phrases within a string printed with surrounding quote marks, simply enter a pair of adjacent quote marks (double quotes) on either side of the particular word or phrase when you type it.

```
>NEW

>100 PRINT "HI!"
>110 PRINT "THIS IS A STRING
 CONSTANT."
>120 PRINT "ALL CHARACTERS (+
 -*/ @,) MAY BE USED."
>130 END
>RUN
 HI!
 THIS IS A STRING CONSTANT.
 ALL CHARACTERS (+-*/ @,) MAY
 BE USED.

 ** DONE **
```

```
>NEW

>100 PRINT "TO PRINT ""QUOTE
 MARKS"" YOU MUST USE DOUBLE
 QUOTES."
>110 PRINT
>120 PRINT "TOM SAID, ""HI, M
 ARY!"""
>130 END
>RUN
 TO PRINT "QUOTE MARKS" YOU M
 UST USE DOUBLE QUOTES.

 TOM SAID, "HI, MARY!"

 ** DONE **
```

Variables

In BASIC all variables are given a name. Each variable name may be one or more characters in length but must begin with a letter, an at-sign (@), a left-bracket ([), a right-bracket (]), a back slash (\), or a line (_). The only characters allowed in a variable name are letters, numbers, the at-sign (@), and the line (_). One exception is the dollar-sign ($). The last character in a string variable name *must* be a dollar-sign ($) and this is the only place in a variable name that it may be used. Variable names are restricted to fifteen characters including the dollar-sign for string variable names.

Array names follow the same rules as simple variable names. (See the section on Arrays for more information.) In a single program, the same name cannot be used both as a simple variable and as an array name, nor can two arrays with different dimensions have the same name. For example, Z and Z(3) cannot both be used as names in the same program, nor can X(3,4) and X(2,1,3). However, there is no relationship between a numeric variable name and a string variable name which agree except for the dollar sign (X and X$ may both be used in the same program).

Numeric Variable Names

Valid: X, A9, ALPHA, BASE_PAY, V(3), T(X,3),
      TABLE (X,XX7Y/2)
Invalid: X$, X/8, 3Y

String Variable Names

Valid: S$, YZ2$, NAME$, Q5$(3, X)
Invalid: S$3, X9, 4Z$

If you enter a variable name with more than fifteen characters, the message "BAD NAME" is displayed and the line is not entered into memory. Reserved words are not allowed as variable names, but may be used as part of a variable name. For example, LIST is not allowed as a variable name but LIST$ is accepted.

At any instant while a program is running, every variable has a single value. When a program begins running, the value associated with each numeric variable is set to zero and the value associated with each string variable is set to null (a string with a length of zero characters). When a program is running, values are assigned to variables when LET statements, READ statements, FOR-TO-STEP statements, or INPUT statements are performed. The length of the character string value associated with a string variable may vary from a length of zero to a limit of 255 characters while a program is running.

Examples:

```
>110 ABCDEFGHIJKLMNOPQ=3

* BAD NAME
```

Numeric Expressions

Numeric expressions are constructed from numeric variables, numeric constants, and function references using arithmetic operators (+ − */ ∧). All functions referenced in an expression must be either functions supplied in TI BASIC (see sections on Built-In Functions) or defined by a DEF statement. The two kinds of arithmetic operators (prefix and infix) are discussed below.

The *prefix* arithmetic operators are plus (+) and minus (−) and are used to indicate the sign (positive or negative) of constants and variables. The plus sign indicates the number following the prefix operator (+) should be multiplied by +1, and the minus sign indicates the number following the prefix operator (−) should be multiplied by −1. Note that if no prefix operator is present, the number is treated as if the prefix operator were plus. Some examples of prefix operators with constants and variables are:

        10   −6   +3
        +A   −W

The *infix* arithmetic operators are used for calculations and include: addition (+), subtraction (−), multiplication (*), division (/), and exponentiation (∧). An infix operator must appear between each numeric constant and/or variable in a numeric expression. Note that multiplication cannot be implied by simply placing variables side by side or by using parentheses. You must use the multiplication operator (*).

Infix and prefix operators may be entered side by side within a numeric expression. The operators are evaluated in the normal way.

Examples:

```
>NEW

>100  A=6
>110  B=4
>120  C=20
>130  D=2
>140  PRINT A*B/2
>150  PRINT C-D*3+6
>160  END
>RUN
   12
   20

  ** DONE **
```

```
>PRINT 3+-1
  2

>PRINT 2*-3
  -6

>PRINT 6/-3
  -2
```

Numeric Expressions

In evaluating numeric expressions, TI BASIC uses the standard rules for mathematical hierarchy. These rules are outlined here.

1. All expressions within parentheses are evaluated first according to the hierarchical rules.
2. Exponentiation is performed next in order from left to right.
3. Prefix plus and minus are performed.
4. Multiplications and divisions are then completed.
5. Additions and subtractions are then completed.

Note that $0 \wedge 0$ is defined to be 1 as in ordinary mathematical usage.

In the evaluation of a numeric expression if an *underflow* occurs, the value is simply replaced by zero and the program continues running. If an *overflow* occurs in the evaluation of a numeric expression, the value is replaced by the computer's limit, a warning condition is indicated by the message "WARNING: NUMBER TOO BIG," and the program continues running.

When evaluation of a numeric expression results in division by zero, the value is replaced by the computer's limit with the same sign as the numerator, the message "WARNING: NUMBER TOO BIG" is displayed, and the program continues running. If the evaluation of the operation of exponentiation results in zero being raised to a negative power, the value is replaced by the positive value of the computer's limit, the message "WARNING: NUMBER TOO BIG" is displayed, and the program continues running. If the evaluation of the operation of exponentiation results in a negative number being raised to a non-integral power, the message "BAD VALUE" is displayed, and the program stops running.

Examples:

```
>NEW

>100 A=2
>110 B=3
>120 C=4
>130 PRINT A*(B+2)
>140 PRINT B^A-4
>150 PRINT -C^A;(-C)^A
>160 PRINT 10-B*C/6
>170 END
>RUN
   10
    5.
  -16   16
    8

** DONE **
```

```
>PRINT 0^0
 1
```

```
>NEW

>100 PRINT 1E-200
>110 PRINT 24+1E-139
>120 PRINT 1E171
>130 PRINT (1E60*1E76)/1E50
>140 END
>RUN
   0
  24

 * WARNING:
   NUMBER TOO BIG IN 120
 9.99999E+**

 * WARNING:
   NUMBER TOO BIG IN 130
 1.E+78

** DONE **
```

```
>NEW

>100 PRINT -22/0
>110 PRINT 0^-2
>120 PRINT (-3)^1.2
>130 END
>RUN

 * WARNING:
   NUMBER TOO BIG IN 100
 -9.99999E+**

 * WARNING:
   NUMBER TOO BIG IN 110
 9.99999E+**

 * BAD VALUE IN 120
```

Relational Expressions

Relational expressions are normally used in the IF-THEN-ELSE statement but may be used anywhere numeric expressions are allowed. When you use relational expressions within a numeric expression, a numeric value of −1 is given if the relation is true and a numeric value of 0 is given if the relation is false.

Relational operations are performed from left to right *before* string concatenation and *after* all arithmetic operations within the expression are completed. To perform string concatenation before relational operations and/or to perform relational operations before arithmetic operations, you must use parentheses. Valid relational operators are:

- Equal to (=)
- Less than (<)
- Greater than (>)
- Not equal to (<>)
- Less than or equal to (< =)
- Greater than or equal to (> =)

An explanation of how string comparisons are performed to give you a true or false result is discussed in the IF-THEN-ELSE explanation. Remember that the result you obtain from the evaluation of a relational operator is always a number. If you try to use the result as a string, you will get an error.

Examples:

```
>NEW

>100 A=2<5
>110 B=3<=2
>120 PRINT A;B
>130 END
>RUN
 -1  0

  ** DONE **


>NEW

>100 A$="HI"
>110 B$=" THERE!"
>120 PRINT (A$&B$)="HI!"
>130 END
>RUN
 0

  ** DONE **

>120 PRINT (A$&B$)>"HI"
>RUN
 -1

  ** DONE **

>120 PRINT (A$>B$)*4
>RUN
 -4

  ** DONE **


>NEW

>100 A=2<4*3
>110 B=A=0
>120 PRINT A;B
>130 END
>RUN
 -1  0

  ** DONE **
```

String Expressions

String expressions are constructed from string variables, string constants, and function references using the operation for concatenation (&). The operation of concatenation allows you to combine strings together. All functions referenced in a string expression must be either functions supplied in TI BASIC (see Built-In String Functions) or defined by a DEF statement and must have a string value. If evaluation of a string expression results in a value which exceeds the maximum string length of 255 characters, the string is truncated on the right, and the program continues running. No warning is given.

Note that all characters included in a string expression are always displayed on the screen exactly as you enter them.

Examples:

```
>NEW

>100 A$="HI"
>110 B$="HELLO THERE!"
>120 C$="HOW ARE YOU?"
>130 MSG$=A$&SEG$(B$,6,7)
>140 PRINT MSG$&" "&C$
>150 END
>RUN
  HI THERE! HOW ARE YOU?

 ** DONE **
```

Reserved Words

Reserved words are words that may not be used as variable names in TI BASIC. Note that only the exact word shown is reserved. You may use reserved words as part of a variable name (for example, ALEN and LENGTH are allowed). The following is a complete list of all reserved words in TI BASIC:

ABS	GOTO	RESEQUENCE
APPEND	IF	RESTORE
ASC	INPUT	RETURN
ATN	INT	RND
BASE	INTERNAL	RUN
BREAK	LEN	SAVE
BYE	LET	SEG$
CALL	LIST	SEQUENTIAL
CHR$	LOG	SGN
CLOSE	NEW	SIN
CON	NEXT	SQR
CONTINUE	NUM	STEP
COS	NUMBER	STOP
DATA	OLD	STR$
DEF	ON	SUB
DELETE	OPEN	TAB
DIM	OPTION	TAN
DISPLAY	OUTPUT	THEN
EDIT	PERMANENT	TO
ELSE	POS	TRACE
END	PRINT	UNBREAK
EOF	RANDOMIZE	UNTRACE
EXP	READ	UPDATE
FIXED	REC	VAL
FOR	RELATIVE	VARIABLE
GO	REM	
GOSUB	RES	

Statements Used as Commands

Many statements in TI BASIC can be entered as commands with no line number. When a statement is entered as a command, it is executed immediately in the normal way (unless there is an error). The following statements may be entered as commands.

CALL
CLOSE
DIMension
DISPLAY
END
LET (assignment)
OPEN
PRINT
RANDOMIZE
REMark
READ
RESTORE
STOP

Commands Used as Statements

Some commands in TI BASIC may be entered as part of a program. Generally, the commands work the same way when they are used as a statement. The following commands may be used in a program.

        BREAK
        UNBREAK
        TRACE
        UNTRACE
        DELETE

Commands

Introduction

Whenever the prompt and flashing cursor (>■) appear at the bottom of your screen, your computer is in Command (Immediate) Mode. When your computer is in Command Mode, you may enter any of the commands discussed in this section. Commands may be typed in and entered without being preceded by a line number. When a command is entered, your computer performs the required task immediately. Many statements may also be entered as commands.

Some of the commands discussed here may be entered as statements. If the command may be entered as a statement, it will be noted in the discussion.

NEW

NEW

The NEW command erases the program that is currently stored in memory. Entering the NEW command cancels the effect of the BREAK command and the TRACE command. The NEW command also closes any open files (see OPEN statement) and releases all space that had been allocated for special characters. In addition, the NEW command erases all variable values and the table in which variable names are stored. After the NEW command is performed, the screen is cleared and the message "TI BASIC READY" is displayed on the screen. The prompt and flashing cursor (> ■) indicate that you may enter another command or a program line.

```
TI BASIC READY
>■
```

LIST

LIST $\left\{ \begin{array}{l} [\textit{line-list}] \\ \textit{"device-name"}[:\textit{line-list}] \end{array} \right\}$

Examples:

When the LIST command is entered, the program lines specified by the *line-list* are displayed. If a *device-name* is entered, then the specified program lines are printed on the specified device. *Device-names* for possible future accessory devices will be given in their respective manuals. If no *device-name* is entered, the specified lines are displayed on the screen.

If the LIST command is entered with no *line-list,* then the entire program is displayed. The program lines are always listed in ascending order. Note that all unnecessary blank spaces that were present when you entered the program line were deleted when the computer accepted the line. Notice that when you list the lines, unnecessary blank spaces have been deleted.

```
>NEW

>100 A=279.3
>120 PRINT A;B
>110 B=-456.8
>130 END
>LIST
 100 A=279.3
 110 B=-456.8
 120 PRINT A;B
 130 END
```

If the *line-list* is entered, it may consist of a single number, a single number preceded by a hyphen (for example: -10), a single number followed by a hyphen (for example: 10-), or a hyphenated range of line numbers. If the *line-list* is:

■ A single number — only the program line for the line number specified is displayed on the screen.

```
>LIST 110
 110 B=-456.8
```

■ A single number preceded by a hyphen — all program lines with line numbers less than or equal to the line number specified are displayed.

```
>LIST -110
 100 A=279.3
 110 B=-456.8
```

■ A single number followed by a hyphen — all program lines with line numbers greater than or equal to the line number specified are displayed.

```
>LIST 120-
 120 PRINT A;B
 130 END
```

■ A hyphenated range of line numbers — all program lines with line numbers not less than the first line number in the range and not greater than the second line number are displayed.

```
>LIST 90-120
 100 A=279.3
 110 B=-456.8
 120 PRINT A;B
```

LIST

If there is a program in memory but there are no program lines within the range specified by the *line-list,* then a program line is displayed according to the following rules. If the *line-list* specifies

■ Line numbers greater than any in the program — the highest numbered program line is displayed.

■ Line numbers less than any in the program — the lowest numbered program line is displayed.

■ Line numbers between lines in the program — the next higher numbered line is displayed.

If you enter a LIST command and specify a line number which is equal to zero or greater than 32767, the message "BAD LINE NUMBER" is displayed.

If you specify a line number which is not an integer, the message "INCORRECT STATEMENT" is displayed.

If no program is in memory when you enter a LIST command, the message "CAN'T DO THAT" is displayed.

When program lines are being displayed after the LIST command has been entered, you can stop the listing by pressing the Break key **(CLEAR)**.

Here is a quick summary of the lines listed when specified in the *line-list.*

Command	Lines Displayed
LIST	All program lines
LIST x	Program line number x
LIST x-y	Program lines between x and y, inclusive
LIST x-	Program lines greater than or equal to x
LIST -y	Program lines less than or equal to y

LIST may also be used to direct output to an accessory device. For example,
      LIST "TP"
causes your program to be printed, if the TI Solid State Thermal Printer is attached, and
      LIST "RS232/1":100-200
outputs program lines 100 to 200 to the TI RS232 Interface. Note that the name of the device must be enclosed in quotation marks. For more information refer to the owner's manual that comes with the accessory device.

Examples:

```
>LIST 150-
 130 END

>LIST -90
 100 A=279.3

>LIST 105
 110 B=-456.8

>LIST 0

 * BAD LINE NUMBER

>LIST 33961

 * BAD LINE NUMBER

>LIST 32.7

 * INCORRECT STATEMENT

>NEW

>LIST

 * CAN'T DO THAT
```

RUN

RUN [*line-number*]

Entering the RUN command causes the program stored in memory to begin running. Before the program starts running, the values of all numeric variables are set to zero, the values of all string variables are set to null (a string of zero characters), and any space previously allocated for special graphics characters is released.

If no *line-number* is specified when the RUN command is entered, then the program starts running at the lowest numbered line in the program.

If a *line-number* is specified when the RUN command is entered, then the program starts running at the specified program line. Note in this example that since the program begins running at line 110, the value of A remains zero.

If you specify a *line-number* which is not in the program, the message "BAD LINE NUMBER" is displayed.

If you enter a RUN command when there is no program in memory, the message "CAN'T DO THAT" is displayed.

Examples:

```
>NEW

>100 A=-16
>110 B=25
>120 PRINT A;B
>130 END
>RUN
 -16   25

 ** DONE **
```

```
>RUN 110
  0   25

 ** DONE **
```

```
>RUN 115

 * BAD LINE NUMBER
```

```
>NEW

>RUN

 * CAN'T DO THAT
```

BYE

BYE

When you are finished working and are ready to leave BASIC,
simply enter the BYE command. We recommend that you always
use the BYE command (instead of **QUIT**) when you wish to leave
BASIC. When the BYE command is entered, the first job your
computer performs is closing all open files (see OPEN
statement). Then, the program in memory and all variable values
are erased. Finally, the computer is reset so that it is ready to go
again when you want to return to BASIC. After the BYE
command is performed, the master computer title screen
reappears.

Examples:

```
>NEW

>100 LET X$="HELLO, GENIUS!"
>110 PRINT X$
>120 END
>RUN
 HELLO, GENIUS!

** DONE **

>BYE

--master computer title
  screen appears
```

NUMBER

$\left\{ \begin{array}{l} \text{NUMBER} \\ \text{NUM} \end{array} \right\}$ [initial-line][,increment]

When the NUMBER command is entered, your computer automatically generates line numbers for you. Your computer is in Number Mode when it is generating line numbers. In Number Mode each line entered in response to a generated line number is added to the program.

The first line number displayed after entering the NUMBER command is the specified *initial-line*. Succeeding line numbers are generated using the specified *increment*. To terminate the automatic generation of line numbers and leave Number Mode, press **ENTER** immediately after the generated line number is displayed. The empty line is not added to the program.

If no *initial-line* and no *increment* are specified, then 100 is used as the *initial-line* and 10 is used as the *increment*.

If you specify only an *initial-line,* then 10 is used as the *increment*.

If you specify just an *increment,* then 100 is used as the *initial-line.* Note the comma before the five in the example. Remember, if you wish to specify only an *increment,* the comma must be typed before the *increment*.

Examples:

```
>NEW

>NUMBER 10,5

>10 C=38.2
>15 D=16.7
>20 PRINT C;D
>25 END
>30 ENTER
>LIST
 10 C=38.2
 15 D=16.7
 20 PRINT C;B
 25 END
```

```
>NEW

>NUM
>100 B$="HELLO!"
>110 PRINT B$
>120 END
>130 ENTER
```

```
>NEW

>NUMBER 50
>50 C$="HI!"
>60 PRINT C$
>70 END
>80 ENTER
```

```
>NEW

>NUM ,5
>100 Z=99.7
>105 PRINT Z
>110 END
>115 ENTER
```

NUMBER

When you are in Number Mode, if a line number generated is already a line in the program, then the existing program line is displayed with the line number. Note that when an existing program line is displayed in Number Mode, the prompt character (>) is not shown to the left of the line number. This indicates the line is an existing program line and you may choose to edit the line. For information on editing, see the section below. If you do not want to change the existing line, simply press **ENTER** when the line is displayed and it will not be changed. After you press **ENTER**, the next line number is generated.

In Number Mode, if you enter a program line and an error occurs, the appropriate error message is displayed as usual and then the same line number is displayed again. Retype the line correctly and then enter it again. If a line number would be generated in Number Mode which is greater than 32767, the computer leaves Number Mode.

Editing in Number Mode

Whether you are entering new lines or changing existing program lines while in Number Mode, all of the special editing keys may be used. Since some of the keys work differently in Number Mode than in Command Mode, the keys and how they work in Number Mode are discussed here.

ENTER — This key has different functions depending on the situation. The functions and situations are described below.

- If you press **ENTER** immediately after a line number is generated, then the computer leaves Number Mode.

- If you type in a statement after the line number is generated and then press **ENTER**, the new line is added to the program. Then the next line number is generated.

- If an existing program line is displayed and you press **ENTER** immediately after it is displayed, the line remains the same in the program. Then the next line number is generated.

- If an existing program line is displayed and you erase the entire text of the line (leaving only the line number on the screen) and then press **ENTER**, the computer leaves Number Mode. The program line is not removed from the program.

- If you edit a line after it is displayed as an existing program line and text still remains after the line number and then press **ENTER**, the existing program line is replaced by the edited line. Then the next line number is generated.

Examples:

```
>NEW

>100 A=37.1
>110 B=49.6
>NUMBER 110
 110 B=49.6
>120 PRINT A;B
>130 END
>140 ENTER
>LIST
 100 A=37.1
 110 B=49.6
 120 PRINT A;B
 130 END
```

NUMBER

FCTN ↑ (UP) — The Up-Arrow key works exactly the same as the **ENTER** key in Number Mode.

FCTN ↓ (DOWN) — The Down-Arrow key works exactly the same as the **ENTER** key in Number Mode.

FCTN ← (LEFT) — The Left-Arrow key moves the cursor one position to the left. When the cursor moves over a character it does not delete or change it in any way.

FCTN → (RIGHT) — The Right-Arrow key moves the cursor one position to the right. Using this key allows you to move the cursor over a character without deleting or changing it in any way.

FCTN 2 (INS) The Insert key works in Number Mode just as it does in Command Mode. See Special Keys for information.

FCTN 1 (DEL) — The Delete key works in Number Mode just as it does in Command Mode. See Special Keys for information.

FCTN 4 (CLEAR) — If you press the Clear key at any time while in Number Mode, the current line scrolls up on the screen and the computer leaves Number Mode. Any changes which had been made on the line before you pressed the Clear key are ignored. Thus, if you were editing an existing program line, the program line does not change. If you were typing in a line, the line is not added to the program.

FCTN 3 (ERASE) — The Erase key erases the entire text of the program line being displayed. The line number is still displayed.

RESEQUENCE

$\begin{cases} \text{RESEQUENCE} \\ \text{RES} \end{cases}$ [initial-line][,increment]

When the RESEQUENCE command is entered, all lines in the program are assigned new line numbers according to the specified *initial-line* and *increment*.

The new line number of the first line in the program is the specified *initial-line*. Succeeding line numbers are assigned using the specified *increment*.

If no *initial-line* and no *increment* are specified, then 100 is used as the *initial-line* and 10 is used as the *increment*.

If you specify only an *initial-line* then 10 is used as the *increment*.

If you specify just an *increment*, then 100 is used as the *initial-line*. Note the comma before the five in the example. Remember, if you wish to specify only an *increment*, the comma must be typed before the *increment*.

All line number references in TI BASIC statements contained in the program are changed to the new line numbers. Line numbers which may be mentioned in the REM statement are not changed since they are not essential to the running of the program.

```
>NEW

>100 A=27.9
>110 B=34.1
>120 PRINT A;B
>130 END

>RESEQUENCE 20,5
>LIST
 20 A=27.9
 25 B=34.1
 30 PRINT A;B
 35 END

>RES
>LIST
 100 A=27.9
 110 B=34.1
 120 PRINT A;B
 130 END

>RES 50
>LIST
 50 A=27.9
 60 B=34.1
 70 PRINT A;B
 80 END

>RES ,5
>LIST
 100 A=27.9
 105 B=34.1
 110 PRINT A;B
 115 END

>NEW

>100 REM THE VALUE OF "A" WIL
L BE PRINTED IN LINE 120
>110 A=A+1
>120 PRINT A
>130 GO TO 110
>RESEQUENCE 10,5
>LIST
 10 REM THE VALUE OF "A" WIL
L BE PRINTED IN LINE 120
 15 A=A+1
 20 PRINT A
 25 GO TO 15
```

RESEQUENCE

If a line number is used in a program line which is not a currently used line number, then the line number reference is changed to 32767. No error or warning is given.

If you enter a value for the *initial-line* and *increment* which would give values greater than 32767 for some new line numbers, the message "BAD LINE NUMBER" is displayed. If this error occurs, no line numbers in the program are changed.

If you enter a RESEQUENCE command while no program is in memory, the message "CAN'T DO THAT" is displayed.

Examples:

```
>NEW

>100 Z=Z+2
>110 PRINT Z
>120 IF Z=50 THEN 150
>130 GO TO 100
>140 END
>RES 10,5
>LIST
 10 Z=Z+2
 15 PRINT Z
 20 IF Z=50 THEN 32767
 25 GO TO 10
 30 END


>RESEQUENCE 32600,100
 * BAD LINE NUMBER

>LIST
 10 Z=Z+2
 15 PRINT Z
 20 IF Z=50 THEN 32767
 25 GO TO 10
 30 END

>NEW

>RESEQUENCE

 * CAN'T DO THAT
```

BREAK

BREAK *line-list*

When the BREAK command is entered, breakpoints are set at the program lines listed in the *line-list*. Breakpoints are usually set to help you find errors in your program. When you set a breakpoint at a specific line using the BREAK command, you tell the computer to stop running the program before performing the statement on that line.

The *line-list* is a list of line numbers where you wish to set breakpoints. The line numbers are separated by commas (for example: BREAK 10,23,35). Of course, you may choose to have only one line number in the list.

Each time a line where a breakpoint is set is reached while the program is running, the program stops running before the statement on that line is performed. When the program stops running because of a breakpoint, the message "BREAKPOINT AT line-number" is displayed, and you are prompted with the flashing cursor to enter a command.

When the program stops running because of a breakpoint, you may enter any command or any statement that can be used as a command. There is no change in the value of the variables unless you enter a statement that will assign a new value. Note that in this example C still equals zero since the assignment in statement 110 has not been performed.

You can start running the program again (beginning with the line where the breakpoint was set) by entering the CONTINUE command. Note the value of A was changed earlier in the example. You cannot enter the CONTINUE command after you have edited the program (added, deleted, or changed program lines). This prevents errors that could result from starting a revised program in the middle. If you enter a CONTINUE command after you have edited the program, the message "CAN'T CONTINUE" is displayed on the screen.

Examples:

```
>NEW

>100 A=26.7
>110 C=19.3
>120 PRINT A
>130 PRINT C
>140 END


>BREAK 110




>RUN

 * BREAKPOINT AT 110

>■


>LIST 110
 110 C=19.3
>PRINT A;C
 26.7  0

>A=5.8

>PRINT A
 5.8


>CONTINUE
 5.8
 19.3

 ** DONE **

>BREAK 120

>RUN

 * BREAKPOINT AT 120

>110 ENTER
>CONTINUE
 * CAN'T CONTINUE
```

BREAK

When a breakpoint is taken (program stops running because of a breakpoint), the breakpoint at that line is removed. Another way to remove breakpoints is to use the UNBREAK command. If a breakpoint is set at a program line and that line is deleted, the breakpoint is also removed. Breakpoints are removed from all program lines when a SAVE command or a NEW command is entered. Note that in the example the breakpoint at 110 was removed when the breakpoint was taken, while the breakpoint at 130 was removed by the UNBREAK command.

Whenever a breakpoint is taken, the standard character set is restored. Thus, any standard characters that had been redefined by CALL CHAR will be converted back to the standard characters. Characters defined in the range 128-159 are unaffected. Note that when this example program is run, a solid bar appears on the screen until the breakpoint is taken. When the breakpoint is taken, the bar becomes a row of asterisks (*) since character 42 is a standard character.

Examples:

```
>110 C=19.3
>RUN
  26.7
  19.3

** DONE **

>BREAK 110,130

>RUN

 * BREAKPOINT AT 110

>UNBREAK

>CONTINUE
  26.7
  19.3

** DONE **

>RUN
  26.7
  19.3

** DONE **


>NEW

>100 CALL CLEAR
>110 CALL CHAR(42,"FFFFFFFFFF
FFFFFF")
>120 CALL HCHAR(12,12,42,10)
>130 FOR I=1 TO 500
>140 NEXT I
>150 END
>BREAK 150

>RUN

 --screen clears

 --solid black line appears
   on screen
```

```
         **********


  * BREAKPOINT AT 150
 >■
```

```
>CONTINUE

** DONE **
```

BREAK

The BREAK command may also be used as a statement in programs. If the BREAK command is entered as a statement with a *line-list,* then breakpoints are set at the line numbers specified. Breakpoints set in this manner may be removed as discussed earlier. Remember, though, when the BREAK command is entered as a statement with a *line-list,* the breakpoints are set again each time the statement is performed.

If the BREAK command is entered as a statement and no *line-list* is specified, then the statement itself acts like a breakpoint. Each time the statement is performed, the program stops running. The only way to keep the program from stopping at a BREAK statement is to delete the line from the program. Note that a BREAK command without a *line-list* may only be entered as a program line.

If you specify a line number in the *line-list* which is equal to zero or greater than 32767, the message "BAD LINE NUMBER" is displayed and the command is ignored (no breakpoints are set at any line specified).

If you specify a line number in the *line-list* which is a valid line number but is not a line in the program, the warning "BAD LINE NUMBER" is displayed. Breakpoints will be set at the lines specified which are program lines.

Examples:

```
>NEW

>100 B=29.7
>110 BREAK 120,140
>120 H=15.8
>130 PRINT B
>140 PRINT H
>150 END
>RUN

  * BREAKPOINT AT 120

>UNBREAK

>CONTINUE
   29.7
   15.8

  ** DONE **


>110 BREAK
>RUN

  * BREAKPOINT AT 110

>CONTINUE
   29.7
   15.8

  ** DONE **

>110 ENTER


>BREAK 120,130140

  * BAD LINE NUMBER

>RUN
   29.7
   15.8

  ** DONE **


>110 BREAK 125,140
>RUN

  * WARNING:
    BAD LINE NUMBER IN 110
   29.7

  * BREAKPOINT AT 140

>CONTINUE
   15.8

  ** DONE **
```

UNBREAK

UNBREAK [*line-list*]

The UNBREAK command is used to remove breakpoints from the program lines listed in the *line-list*. For an explanation of breakpoints and how they are set, see the BREAK command.

The *line-list* is a list of line numbers where you want to remove breakpoints. The line numbers are separated by commas. (For example: UNBREAK 10,23.) If you specify only one line number in the *line-list*, no commas are needed.

If you enter an UNBREAK command with no *line-list*, then all breakpoints which have been set by a BREAK command or statement are removed. Note that the UNBREAK command has no effect on a BREAK statement with no *line-list*. The only way to keep the program from stopping at a BREAK statement with no *line-list* is to delete the line.

The UNBREAK command may also be used as a statement in a program. The UNBREAK statement is performed just like the UNBREAK command. Note in the example, the UNBREAK statement removed the breakpoint that was set at 130.

Examples:

```
>NEW

>100 A=26.7
>110 C=19.3
>120 PRINT A
>130 PRINT C
>140 END
>BREAK 110,130

>RUN

 * BREAKPOINT AT 110

>UNBREAK 130

>CONTINUE
  26.7
  19.3

 ** DONE **

>125 BREAK
>BREAK 100,120,130

>RUN

 * BREAKPOINT AT 100
>UNBREAK

>CONTINUE
  26.7

 * BREAKPOINT AT 125

>CONTINUE
  19.3

 ** DONE **


>BREAK 130

>125 UNBREAK 130
>RUN
  26.7
  19.3

 ** DONE **

>125 ENTER
```

UNBREAK

If you specify a line number in the *line-list* which is equal to zero or greater than 32767, the message "BAD LINE NUMBER" is displayed and the command is ignored (no breakpoints are removed at any line specified).

If you specify a line number in the *line-list* which is a valid line number but is not a line in the program, the warning "BAD LINE NUMBER" is displayed. Breakpoints are removed at the lines specified which are program lines.

Examples:

```
>BREAK 130

>UNBREAK 130,110150

 * BAD LINE NUMBER

>RUN
  26.7

 * BREAKPOINT AT 130

>CONTINUE
  19.3

 ** DONE **
```

```
>BREAK 130

>UNBREAK 130,105

 * WARNING:
   BAD LINE NUMBER

>RUN
  26.7
  19.3

 ** DONE **
```

CONTINUE

{CONTINUE }
{CON   }

The CONTINUE command may be entered whenever the program stops running because of a breakpoint. For an explanation of breakpoints and how they are set, see the BREAK command. Remember that a breakpoint is also taken when the Break key **(CLEAR)** is pressed while the program is running.

You cannot enter the CONTINUE command when the program has stopped running for a breakpoint if you have edited the program (added, deleted, or changed program lines). This prevents errors that could result from starting a revised program in the middle. If you enter a CONTINUE command after you have edited the program, the message "CAN'T CONTINUE" is displayed on the screen.

Whenever a breakpoint is taken, the standard character set is restored. Thus, any standard characters that had been redefined by CALL CHAR will be converted back to the standard characters. Characters defined in the range 128-159 are unaffected. If you continue execution after a breakpoint, the standard character set is used. Note in the example that character 42 was defined in statement 110 to be a solid block; however, when the breakpoint was taken, it was changed back to its standard character, an asterisk (*). The triangle defined for character code 128 is unaffected by the breakpoint.

Examples:
```
>NEW

>100 A=9.6
>110 PRINT A
>120 END
>BREAK 110

>RUN

 * BREAKPOINT AT 110
>CONTINUE
   9.6

 ** DONE **

>BREAK 110

>RUN

 * BREAKPOINT AT 110

>100 A=10.1
>CONTINUE
 * CAN'T CONTINUE


>NEW


>100 CALL CLEAR
>110 CALL CHAR(42,"FFFFFFFFFF
 FFFFFF")
>120 CALL CHAR(128,"0103070F1F
 3F7FFF")
>130 CALL HCHAR(10,10,42,5)
>140 CALL HCHAR(11,10,128,5)
>150 FOR I=1 to 500
>160 NEXT I
>170 END
>BREAK 130

>RUN

 * BREAKPOINT AT 130

>CONTINUE


      *****
      ▲▲▲▲▲

 ** DONE **
```

TRACE

TRACE

The TRACE command allows you to see the order in which the computer performs statements as it runs a program. After the TRACE command is entered, the line number of each program line is displayed before the statement is performed. The TRACE command is most often used to help find errors, such as unwanted infinite loops, in a program.

The TRACE command may be placed as a statement in a program. The effect of the TRACE command or statement is cancelled when the NEW command or UNTRACE command or statement is performed.

```
>NEW

>100 PRINT "HI"
>110 B=27.9
>120 PRINT :B
>130 END
>TRACE

>RUN
 <100>HI
 <110><120>
  27.9
 <130>
** DONE **

>UNTRACE

>105 TRACE
>RUN
 HI
 <110><120>
  27.9
 <130>
** DONE **
```

UNTRACE

UNTRACE

The UNTRACE command cancels the effect of the TRACE command. The UNTRACE command may be used as a statement in a program.

Examples:

```
>NEW

>100 FOR I=1 TO 2
>110 PRINT I
>120 NEXT I
>130 END
>TRACE

>RUN
 <100><110> 1
 <120><110> 2
 <120><130>
 ** DONE **

>UNTRACE

>RUN
 1
 2

 ** DONE **
```

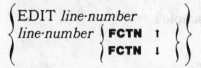

EDIT

$$\left\{\begin{array}{l} \text{EDIT } \textit{line-number} \\ \textit{line-number } \left\{\begin{array}{l} \textbf{FCTN } \uparrow \\ \textbf{FCTN } \downarrow \end{array}\right\} \end{array}\right\}$$

Existing program lines may be changed by entering Edit Mode. You can enter Edit Mode by entering the EDIT command followed by a *line-number* or by typing in a *line-number* followed by **FCTN** ↑ (Up-Arrow) or **FCTN** ↓ (Down-Arrow). Either way you choose to enter Edit Mode will bring the line specified by the *line-number* onto the screen. If you specify a *line-number* which is not in the program, the message "BAD LINE NUMBER" is displayed.

When you enter Edit Mode, the program line you requested is displayed on the screen. The prompt character (>) is not displayed to the left of the line when you are in Edit Mode. When the requested line is displayed, the flashing cursor is positioned in the second character position to the right of the line number. Changes may be made to any character on the line except the line number using the special keys described below and typing over the characters you wish to change. You cannot move the cursor back over the line number. Thus, you cannot change the line number in Edit Mode. The special editing keys and their functions in Edit Mode are discussed here.

ENTER — When you press the **ENTER** key, all changes you have made to the program line become permanent and the computer leaves Edit Mode. If you have erased the entire text of the program line and then press **ENTER**, the program line is deleted. Note that the cursor does not have to be at the end of the line for the entire line to be entered.

FCTN ↑ (UP) — When you press the Up-Arrow key, all changes you have made to the program line are entered and become permanent. The next lower numbered line in the program is then displayed for editing. If no lower numbered program line exists, then the computer leaves Edit Mode. Note that the cursor does not have to be at the end of the line for the entire line to be entered by the Up-Arrow key.

FCTN ↓ (DOWN) — When you press the Down-Arrow key, all changes you have made to the program line are entered and become permanent. The next higher numbered program line is then displayed for editing. If no higher numbered program line exists, then the computer leaves Edit Mode. Note that the cursor does not have to be at the end of the line for the entire line to be entered by the Down-Arrow key.

EDIT

FCTN ← (LEFT) — The Left-Arrow (backspace) key moves the cursor one position to the left. When the cursor moves over a character it does not delete or change it in any way.

FCTN → (RIGHT) — The Right-Arrow (forwardspace) key moves the cursor one position to the right. Using this key allows you to move the cursor over a character without deleting or changing it in any way.

FCTN 2 (INS) — The Insert key works in Edit Mode just as it does in Command Mode. See Special Keys for information.

FCTN 1 (DEL) — The Delete key works in Edit Mode just as it does in Command Mode. See Special Keys for information.

FCTN 4 (CLEAR) — If you press the Clear key at any time while in Edit Mode, the current line scrolls up on the screen and the computer leaves Edit Mode. Any changes which had been made on the line before you pressed the Clear key are ignored. Thus, the existing program line does not change.

FCTN 3 (ERASE) — The Erase key erases the entire text of the program line currently displayed for editing. The line number is not erased.

SAVE

SAVE *file-name*

The SAVE command allows you to copy the current program in the computer's memory onto an accessory device. By using the OLD command, you can later put the program into memory for running or editing.

A brief explanation of using a cassette recorder as a storage device is given here. (For a more detailed discussion, see the "Cassette Interface Cable" section of this manual.) Instructions for using the TI Disk Memory System are given in the owner's manual that accompanies the TI Disk Drive Controller.

You select which cassette recorder the computer will use by entering the *file-name* CS1 or CS2 following the keyword SAVE. After you have connected your recorder to the computer, type the SAVE command, and press **ENTER.** The computer then begins printing instructions on the screen to help you understand the SAVE procedures. Follow the directions as they appear on the screen.

On the right are the computer-generated SAVE instructions. CS1 is used in the example, but the same procedures apply for CS2 also.

When you enter the SAVE command, the computer tells you how to use the recorder, as shown on the right. After the program has been copied, the computer asks if you want to check the tape to be sure your program was recorded correctly. If you press **N**, the flashing cursor will appear at the left of the screen. You may then type any BASIC command you wish. If you press **Y**, directions for activating the recorder will appear.

Note: The single-letter responses (**Y, N, R,** etc.) you give during the SAVE routine must be upper-case characters. Hold down the **SHIFT** key, and press the appropriate letter key.

```
>SAVE CS1

 * REWIND CASSETTE TAPE    CS1
   THEN PRESS ENTER

 * PRESS CASSETTE RECORD   CS1
   THEN PRESS ENTER

 * RECORDING

 * PRESS CASSETTE STOP     CS1
   THEN PRESS ENTER

 * CHECK TAPE (Y OR N)? Y

 * REWIND CASSETTE TAPE    CS1
   THEN PRESS ENTER

 * PRESS CASSETTE PLAY     CS1
   THEN PRESS ENTER

 * CHECKING

 * DATA OK

 * PRESS CASSETTE STOP     CS1
   THEN PRESS ENTER
```

an error occurred, you may choose one of these three options:

- Press **R** to record your program again. The same instructions listed previously will guide you.

- Press **C** to repeat the checking procedures. At this point you may wish to adjust the recorder volume and/or tone controls.

- Press **E** to "exit" from the recording procedure. The computer will tell you to stop the cassette and press **ENTER.** You will see an error message on the screen. This means that the SAVE routine did not properly record your program. After checking your recorder, you can try to record the program again. When the flashing cursor reappears on the screen, enter any BASIC command you wish.

When the SAVE command is performed, whether or not an error occurred in recording, the program remains in memory.

Examples:

```
* ERROR - NO DATA FOUND
  PRESS R TO RECORD
  PRESS C TO CHECK
  PRESS E TO EXIT

          or

* ERROR IN DATA DETECTED
  PRESS R TO RECORD
  PRESS C TO CHECK
  PRESS E TO EXIT

* I/O ERROR 66
```

OLD

OLD *file-name*

The OLD command copies a previously SAVEd program into the computer's memory. You can then run, list, or change the program. An explanation for using the audio cassette tape recorder (CS1) with the OLD command is given here. Instructions concerning the TI Disk Memory System are given in the owner's manual that accompanies the TI Disk Drive Controller.

After you type the OLD command and press **ENTER**, the computer will begin printing instructions on the screen to help you through the procedures. Follow the directions as they appear on the screen. Be sure you have connected the recorder and inserted the proper cassette tape.

On the right are the instructions displayed on the screen when you enter the OLD command. You will find a detailed description of these procedures in the "Cassette Interface Cable" section of this book.

If the computer did not successfully read your program into memory, an error occurs and you may choose either of these options:

■ Press **R** to repeat the reading procedure. Before repeating the procedure, be sure to check the items listed in the "Cassette Interface" section.

■ Press **E** to "exit" from the reading procedure. An error message indicating that the computer did not properly read your program into memory is displayed.

Note: The single-letter responses (**E** or **R**) you give during the OLD routine must be upper-case characters. Hold down the **SHIFT** key, and press the appropriate letter key.

When the flashing cursor reappears on the screen, you may enter any BASIC command you wish.

Even though the program has not been successfully read into the computer's memory, it may overwrite part or all of any program that was previously in memory. You may want to LIST and check the memory contents before going on.

Examples:

```
>OLD CS1

* REWIND CASSETTE TAPE    CS1
  THEN PRESS ENTER

* PRESS CASSETTE PLAY     CS1
  THEN PRESS ENTER

* READING

* DATA OK

* PRESS CASSETTE STOP     CS1
  THEN PRESS ENTER

          or

* ERROR - NO DATA FOUND
  PRESS R TO READ
  PRESS E TO EXIT

* I/O ERROR 56
```

DELETE

DELETE $\left\{ \begin{array}{l} \textit{file-name} \\ \textit{program-name} \end{array} \right\}$

The DELETE command allows you to remove a program or a data file from a diskette. The *file-name* and *program-name* are string expressions. If a string constant is used, you must enclose it in quotes.

You may also remove data files from the computer system by using the keyword DELETE in the CLOSE statement. The action performed depends upon the device used. See the owner's manual enclosed with the TI Disk Drive Controller for additional information.

If you use DELETE with cassette tape recorders, no action occurs. The message on the right will appear on the screen.

```
>SAVE DSK1.DATA
>DELETE "DSK1.DATA"
```

```
>500 CLOSE #7:DELETE
```

```
>DELETE "CS1"
```

```
* PRESS CASSETTE STOP     CS1
  THEN PRESS ENTER
```

General Program Statements

Introduction

This section describes those general program statements that do not serve an input-output function. They include the LET statement, which allows you to assign values to variables, the STOP, END, and REMark statements, and those statements which control the path the computer takes when it runs your program. These program control statements, including the GOTO, the ON-GOTO, the IF-THEN-ELSE, the FOR-TO-STEP, and the NEXT statements, allow you to easily program loops and conditional and unconditional branches. By using the statements in this section and in the Input-Output section, you can write enjoyable, useful programs.

LET (Assignment Statement)

[LET] *variable = expression*

The LET statement allows you to assign values to variables in your program. The computer evaluates the *expression* to the right of the equals sign and puts its value into the *variable* specified to the left of the equals sign.

The *variable* and the *expression* must correspond in type: numeric expressions must be assigned to numeric variables; string expressions must be assigned to string variables. The rules governing overflow and underflow for the evaluation of a numeric expression are used in the LET statement. See "Numeric Constants" for a full explanation. If the length of an evaluated string expression exceeds 255 characters, the string is truncated on the right, and the program continues. No warning is given.

You may use relational operators in numeric and string expressions. The result of a relational operator is –1 if the relationship is true and is 0 if the relationship is false.

Examples:

```
>NEW

>100 LET M=1000
>110 LET C=186000
>120 E=M*C^2
>130 PRINT E
>140 END
>RUN
   3.4596E+13

 ** DONE **
```

```
>NEW

>100 LET X$="HELLO, "
>110 NAME$="GENIUS!"
>120 PRINT X$;NAME$
>130 END
>RUN
 HELLO, GENIUS!

 ** DONE **
```

```
>NEW

>100 LET A=20
>110 B=10
>120 LET C=A>B
>130 PRINT A;B;C
>140 C=A<B
>150 PRINT A;B;C
>160 END
>RUN
   20   10 -1
   20   10  0

 ** DONE **
```

REMark

REM *remark*

The REMark statement allows you to explain and document your program by inserting comments in the program itself. When the computer encounters a REMark statement while running your program, it takes no action but proceeds to the next statement.

You may use any printable character in a REMark statement. The length of the REMark statement is limited by the length of the input line (112 characters or four lines on the screen). If you do not wish to break a word in the middle, press the space bar repeatedly until the cursor returns to the left side of the screen, and then you may begin typing again.

Examples:

```
>NEW

>100 REM COUNTING FROM 1 TO
 10
>110 FOR X=1 TO 10
>120 PRINT X;
>130 NEXT X
>140 END
>RUN
  1 2 3 4 5 6 7 8 9
  10
 ** DONE **
```

```
>NEW

>100 A=762
>110 B=425
>120 REM NOW PRINT THE SUM OF
 A AND B
>130 PRINT A+B
>140 END
>RUN
  1187

 ** DONE **
```

END

END

The END statement terminates your program when it is being run and may be used interchangeably with the STOP statement in TI BASIC. Although the END statement can appear anywhere in the program, it is normally placed at the last line number in the program and thus ends the program both physically and logically. Although you may place END statements anywhere in your program, the STOP statement is usually used if you want to have other termination points in your program. In TI BASIC you are not required to place an END statement in the program.

Examples:

```
>NEW

>100 A=10
>110 B=20
>120 C=A*B
>130 PRINT C
>140 END
>RUN
   200

 ** DONE **
```

STOP

STOP

The STOP statement terminates your program when it is being run and can be used interchangeably with the END statement in TI BASIC. You can place STOP statements anywhere in your program and use several STOP statements in the same program. Many BASIC programmers use the END statement if there is only one ending point in the program.

```
>NEW

>100 A=5
>110 B$="TEXAS INSTRUMENTS"
>120 PRINT B$;A
>130 STOP
>RUN
  TEXAS INSTRUMENTS 5

** DONE **


>NEW

>100 CALL CLEAR
>110 FOR I=1 TO 15
>120 CALL HCHAR(1,1,42,768)
>130 GOSUB 160
>140 NEXT I
>150 STOP
>160 F=I
>170 B=I+1
>180 CALL COLOR(2,F,B)
>190 RETURN
>200 END
>RUN

  --SCREEN WILL FILL WITH
    ASTERISKS AND CHANGE
    COLORS 15 TIMES

** DONE **
```

GOTO

$\left\{ \begin{array}{l} \text{GOTO} \\ \text{GO TO} \end{array} \right\}$ *line-number*

The GOTO statement allows you to transfer control backward or forward within a program. Whenever the computer reaches a GOTO statement, it will always jump to the statement with the specified *line-number*. This is called an *unconditional* branch.

In the program on the right, line 170 is an *unconditional* branch. The computer always skips to line 140 at this point. Line 160 is a *conditional* branch (see "IF-THEN-ELSE"). The computer jumps to line 180 only if COUNT and DAYS are equal.

If you should tell the computer to skip to a *line-number* that does not exist in your program, the program will stop running and print the message "BAD LINE NUMBER."

Note that the space between the words GO and TO is optional.

Examples:

```
>NEW
>100 REM HOW MANY GIFTS ON
 THE 12 DAYS OF CHRISTMAS?
>110 GIFTS=0
>120 DAYS=1
>130 COUNT=0
>140 COUNT=COUNT+1
>150 GIFTS=GIFTS+1
>160 IF COUNT=DAYS THEN 180
>170 GOTO 140
>180 DAYS=DAYS+1
>190 IF DAYS<=12 THEN 130
>200 PRINT "TOTAL NUMBER OF G
 IFTS IS";GIFTS
>210 END
>RUN
 TOTAL NUMBER OF GIFTS IS 78

** DONE **
```

ON-GOTO

ON *numeric-expression* $\left\{ \begin{array}{l} \text{GOTO} \\ \text{GO TO} \end{array} \right\}$ *line-number* [,*line-number*]...

The ON-GOTO statement tells the computer to jump to one of several program lines, depending on the value of the *numeric-expression*.

The computer first evaluates the *numeric-expression* and rounds the result to an integer. This integer then becomes a pointer for the computer, indicating which program line in the ON-GOTO statement to perform next. If the value of the *numeric-expression* is 1, the computer will proceed to the statement with the first *line-number* specified in the ON-GOTO statement. If the value is 2, the computer will branch to the statement with the second *line-number* listed in the ON-GOTO statement, and so on.

If the rounded value of the *numeric-expression* is less than 1 or greater than the number of *line-numbers* listed in the ON-GOTO statement, the program will stop running and print "BAD VALUE IN xx." If the *line-number* you specify is outside the range of line numbers in your program, the message "BAD LINE NUMBER" is displayed and the program stops running.

Examples:

```
>NEW

>100 REM HOW DOES ON-GOTO
 WORK?
>110 INPUT X
>120 ON X GOTO 130,150,170,19
 0,210
>130 PRINT "X=1"
>140 GOTO 110
>150 PRINT "X=2"
>160 GOTO 110
>170 PRINT "X=3"
>180 GOTO 110
>190 PRINT "X=4"
>200 GOTO 110
>210 END
>RUN
 ? 2
 X=2
 ? 1.2
 X=1
 ? 3.7
 X=4
 ? 6

 * BAD VALUE IN 120
```

IF-THEN-ELSE

IF $\left\{ \begin{array}{l} \textit{relational-expression} \\ \textit{numeric-expression} \end{array} \right\}$ THEN *line-1* [ELSE *line-2*]

The IF-THEN-ELSE statement allows you to change the normal sequence of your program execution by using a *conditional* branch.

The computer evaluates the expression you have included in the statement, such as A>50. If the expression is true, the computer will jump to *line-1,* which follows the word THEN. If the condition is false, the computer will jump to *line-2* following the word ELSE. If ELSE is omitted, the computer continues with the next program line.

In an IF-THEN-ELSE statement, a value of 0 is treated as false, and any other value is treated as true. Thus, you can use multiplication as a *logical-AND* and addition as a *logical-OR*. For example,

IF (A<B)*(C<D) THEN 1000

will go to line 1000 if A is less than B and C is less than D.

The allowable relational operators in TI BASIC are:

- equal to (=)
- less than (<)
- greater than (>)
- not equal to (<>)
- less than or equal to (<=)
- greater than or equal to (>=)

Here are some valid relationship tests:

- A>7
- A$<"YES"
- (A+B)/2<>AVG
- CHR$(L)="A"
- (A$&C$)>=D$

A *numeric-expression* must be compared to another *numeric-expression* and a *string-expression* to another *string-expression*. *Numeric-expressions* are compared algebraically. *String-expressions* are compared left-to-right, character by character, using the ASCII character codes. A character with a lower ASCII code will be considered less than one with a higher ASCII code. Thus, you can sort strings into numeric or alphabetic order. If one string is longer than the other, the comparison is made for each character in the shorter string. If there is no difference, the computer considers the longer string to be greater.

IF-THEN-ELSE

An alternative format of the IF-THEN-ELSE statement is to use a *numeric-expression* with no relationship expressed. In the example on the right, the computer will evaluate the expression $A+B$. If the result is zero, the expression is treated as false. A non-zero result is treated as true. This is the same as:

$$\text{IF } expression <> 0 \text{ THEN } line\text{-}1.$$

Examples:

```
>NEW

>100 INPUT "A IS ":A
>110 INPUT "B IS ":B
>120 IF A+B THEN 150
>130 PRINT "RESULT IS ZERO,EX
 PRESSION FALSE"
>140 GOTO 100
>150 PRINT "RESULT IS NON-ZER
 O,EXPRESSION TRUE"
>160 GO TO 100
>RUN
 A IS 2
 B IS 3
 RESULT IS NON-ZERO,EXPRESSIO
 N TRUE
 A IS 2
 B IS -2
 RESULT IS ZERO,EXPRESSION FA
 LSE
```

(Press **CLEAR** to end loop)

FOR-TO-STEP

FOR *control-variable=initial-value* TO *limit* [STEP *increment*]

The FOR-TO-STEP statement is used for easy programming of repetitive (iterative) processes. Together with the NEXT statement, the FOR-TO-STEP statement is used to construct a FOR-NEXT loop. If the STEP clause is omitted, the computer uses an *increment* of +1.

The *control-variable* is a numeric variable which acts as a counter for the loop. When the FOR-TO-STEP statement is performed, the *control-variable* is set to the *initial-value*. The computer then performs program statements until it encounters a NEXT statement.

When the NEXT statement is performed, the computer increments the *control-variable* by the amount specified in the STEP clause. (When the *increment* is a negative value, the *control-variable* is actually reduced by the STEP amount.) The computer then compares the *control-variable* to the value of the *limit*. If the *control-variable* does not yet exceed the *limit,* the computer repeats the statements following the FOR-TO-STEP statement until the NEXT statement is again encountered and performed. If the new value for the *control-variable* is greater than the *limit* (if the *increment* is positive) or less than the *limit* (if the *increment* is negative), the computer leaves the loop and continues with the program statement following the NEXT statement. The value of the *control-variable* is not changed when the computer leaves the FOR-NEXT loop.

You control the number of times the FOR-NEXT loop is performed by the values you assign in the FOR-TO-STEP statement. The *limit,* and, optionally, the STEP *increment* are numeric-expressions that are evaluated once during a loop performance (when the FOR-TO-STEP statement is encountered) and remain in effect until the loop is finished. Any change made to these values while a loop is in progress has no effect on the number of times the loop is performed. If the value of the *increment* is zero, the computer displays the error message "BAD VALUE IN xx" and the program stops running.

Examples:

```
>NEW

>100 REM COMPUTING SIMPLE
 INTEREST FOR 10 YEARS
>110 INPUT "PRINCIPLE? ":P
>120 INPUT "RATE? ":R
>130 FOR YEARS=1 TO 10
>140 P=P+(P*R)
>150 NEXT YEARS
>160 P=INT(P*100+.5)/100
>170 PRINT P
>180 END
>RUN
 PRINCIPLE? 100
 RATE? .0775
 210.95

** DONE **
```

```
>NEW

>100 REM EXAMPLE OF
 FRACTIONAL INCREMENT
>110 FOR X=.1 TO 1 STEP .2
>120 PRINT X;
>130 NEXT X
>140 PRINT :X
>150 END
>RUN
 .1  .3  .5  .7  .9
 1.1

** DONE **
```

```
>NEW

>100 L=5
>110 FOR I=1 TO L
>120 L=20
>130 PRINT L;I
>140 NEXT I
>150 END
>RUN
 20   1
 20   2
 20   3
 20   4
 20   5

** DONE **
```

FOR-TO-STEP

After you enter a RUN command, but before your program is performed, the computer checks to see that you have the same number of FOR-TO-STEP and NEXT statements. If you do not have the same number, the message "FOR-NEXT ERROR" is displayed and the program is not run.

If you change the value of the *control-variable* while the loop is performed, the number of times the loop is repeated is affected.

```
>NEW

>100 FOR I=1 TO 10
>110 I=I+1
>120 PRINT I
>130 NEXT I
>140 PRINT I
>150 END
>RUN
  2
  4
  6
  8
  10
  11

 ** DONE **
```

In TI BASIC the expressions for *initial-value, limit,* and *increment* are evaluated before the *initial-value* is assigned to the *control-variable*. Thus, in the program on the right, in line 110 the value 5 is assigned to the *limit* before assigning a value to I as the *control-variable*. The loop is repeated 5 times, not just once.

```
>NEW

>100 I=5
>110 FOR I=1 TO I
>120 PRINT I;
>130 NEXT I
>140 END
>RUN
  1  2  3  4  5
 ** DONE **
```

The sign of the *control-variable* can change during the performance of a FOR-NEXT loop.

```
>NEW

>100 FOR I=2 TO -3 STEP -1
>110 PRINT I;
>120 NEXT I
>130 END
>RUN
  2  1  0 -1 -2 -3
 ** DONE **
```

When performing the FOR statement, the computer checks that the *limit* exceeds the *initial-value* before it does the loop. The *initial-value* in the FOR statement does *not* have to be 1. The computer can begin counting with whatever numeric value you wish. However, if the *initial-value* is greater than the *limit* and the *increment* is positive, the loop will not be performed at all. The computer will continue on to the statement following the loop. Similarly, if the *increment* is negative and you assign an *initial-value* less than the *limit,* the loop will not be performed.

```
>NEW

>100 REM INITIAL VALUE TOO
 GREAT
>110 FOR I=6 TO 5
>120 PRINT I
>130 NEXT I
>140 END
>RUN

 ** DONE **
```

FOR-TO-STEP

FOR-NEXT loops may be "nested"; that is, one FOR-NEXT loop may be contained wholly within another. You must use caution, however, to observe the following conventions:

- Each FOR-TO-STEP statement must be paired with a NEXT statement.
- Different *control-variables* must be used for each nested FOR-NEXT loop.
- If a FOR-NEXT loop contains any portion of another FOR-NEXT loop, it must contain *all* of the second FOR-NEXT loop.

Otherwise, the computer will stop running your program and print the error message "CAN'T DO THAT IN xx" if a FOR-NEXT loop overlaps another.

You may branch out of a FOR-NEXT loop using GOTO and IF-THEN-ELSE statements, but you may not branch into a FOR-NEXT loop using these statements. You may use GOSUB statements to leave a FOR-NEXT loop and return. Be sure you do not use the same *control-variable* for any FOR-NEXT loops you may have in your subroutines.

```
>NEW

>100 REM FIND THE LOWEST
THREE DIGIT NUMBER EQUAL TO
THE SUM OF THE CUBES OF ITS
DIGITS
>110 FOR HUND=1 TO 9
>120 FOR TENS=0 TO 9
>130 FOR UNITS=0 TO 9
>140 SUM=100*HUND+10*TENS+UNI
TS
>150 IF SUM<>HUND^3+TENS^3+UN
ITS^3 THEN 180
>160 PRINT SUM
>170 GOTO 210
>180 NEXT UNITS
>190 NEXT TENS
>200 NEXT HUND
>210 END
>RUN
   153

** DONE **


>NEW

>100 FOR I=1 TO 3
>110 PRINT I
>120 GOSUB 140
>130 NEXT I
>140 FOR I=1 TO 5
>150 PRINT I;
>160 NEXT I
>170 RETURN
>180 END
>RUN
   1
   1  2  3  4  5
 * CAN'T DO THAT IN 130
```

NEXT

NEXT *control-variable*

The NEXT statement is always paired with the FOR-TO-STEP statement for construction of a loop. The *control-variable* is the same one that appears in the corresponding FOR-TO-STEP statement.

The NEXT statement actually controls whether the computer will repeat the loop or exit to the program line following the NEXT statement.

When the computer encounters the NEXT statement, it adds the previously evaluated *increment* in the STEP clause to the *control-variable*. It then tests the *control-variable* to see if it exceeds the previously evaluated *limit* specified in the FOR-TO-STEP statement. If the *control-variable* does not exceed the *limit,* the loop is repeated.

Examples:

```
>NEW

>100 REM COUNTING FROM 1 TO
 10
>110 FOR X=1 TO 10
>120 PRINT X;
>130 NEXT X
>140 END
>RUN
  1  2  3  4  5  6  7  8  9
 10
 ** DONE **
```

```
>NEW

>100 REM ROCKET COUNTDOWN
>110 CALL CLEAR
>120 FOR I=10 TO 1 STEP -1
>130 PRINT I
>140 FOR DELAY=1 TO 200
>150 NEXT DELAY
>160 CALL CLEAR
>170 NEXT I
>180 PRINT "BLAST OFF!"
>190 REM CHANGE SCREEN COLOR
>200 FOR COLOR=2 TO 16 STEP 2
>210 CALL SCREEN(COLOR)
>220 FOR DELAY=1 TO 100
>230 NEXT DELAY
>240 NEXT COLOR
>250 END
>RUN

--computer will flash countdow

 BLAST OFF!

--screen will change color
  8 times

 ** DONE **
```

Input-Output Statements

Introduction

INPUT-OUTPUT statements allow you to transfer data in and out of your program. This section describes these statements (PRINT, DISPLAY, INPUT, READ, DATA, RESTORE) as they are used with your TI computer keyboard and screen.

Data can be input to your program from three types of sources:

- from the keyboard — using the INPUT statement
- internally from the program itself — using the READ, DATA, and RESTORE statements
- from files stored on accessory devices — using the INPUT statement

Data can go to two types of output devices:

- the screen — using the PRINT or DISPLAY statements
- files stored on accessory devices — using the PRINT statement

There are two other sections in this Reference Guide which describe additional input-output capabilities of the TI computer. The "File Processing" section helps you construct the statements used with accessory devices. And, since your TI computer is enhanced by graphics, color, and sound, many built-in subprograms also serve an input-output function. The "Color Graphics and Sound" section shows you how to use these features.

INPUT

INPUT [*input-prompt:*] *variable-list*

(For information on the use of the INPUT statement with a file, see the "File Processing" section.)

This form of the INPUT statement is used when entering data via the keyboard. The INPUT statement causes the program to pause until valid data is entered from the keyboard. Although the computer usually accepts up to one input line (4 lines on your screen) for each INPUT statement, a long list of values may be rejected by the computer. If you receive the message "LINE TOO LONG" after entering an input line, you will need to divide the lengthy INPUT statement into at least two separate statements.

Entering the Input Statement

The *input-prompt* is a string expression that indicates on the screen the values you should enter at that time. Including an *input-prompt* in the INPUT statement is optional. When the computer performs an INPUT statement that does not have an *input-prompt*, it displays a question mark (?) followed by a space and waits for you to enter your data.

If you use an *input-prompt*, the string expression must be followed by a colon. When the computer performs this type of INPUT statement, it will display the *input-prompt* message on the screen and wait for you to enter your data.

The *variable-list* contains those variables which are assigned values when the INPUT statement is performed. Variable names in the *variable-list* are separated by commas and may be numeric and/or string variables.

Examples:

```
>NEW
>100 INPUT B
>110 PRINT B
>120 END
>RUN
  ? 25
  25

** DONE **
```

```
>NEW
>100 INPUT "COST OF CAR?":B
>110 A$="TAX?"
>120 INPUT A$:C
>130 INPUT "SALES "&A$:X
>140 PRINT B;C;X
>150 END
 RUN
 COST OF CAR?5500
 TAX?500
 SALES TAX?500
  5500  500  500

** DONE **
```

```
>NEW
>100 INPUT A,B$,C,D
>110 PRINT A:B$:C:D
>120 END
 RUN
 ? 10,HELLO,25,3.2
  10
 HELLO
  25
  3.2

** DONE **
```

INPUT

Responding to an Input Statement

When an INPUT statement is performed, the values corresponding to the variables must be entered in the same order as they are listed in the INPUT statement. When you enter the values, they must all be entered in one input line (up to 4 screen lines) with the values separated by commas. When inputting string values, you may enclose the string in quotes. However, if the string you wish to input contains a comma, a leading quote mark, leading spaces, or trailing spaces, it *must* be enclosed in quotes.

Variables are assigned values from left to right in the *variable-list*. Thus, subscript expressions in the *variable-list* are not evaluated until variables to the left have been assigned values.

Examples:

```
>NEW

>100 INPUT A$
>110 PRINT A$::
>120 INPUT B$
>130 PRINT B$::
>140 INPUT C$
>150 PRINT C$::
>160 INPUT D$
>170 X=500
>180 PRINT D$;X::
>190 INPUT E$
>200 PRINT E$
>210 END
 RUN
 ? "JONES, MARY"
 JONES, MARY

 ? """HELLO THERE"""
 "HELLO THERE"

 ? "JAMES B. SMITH, JR."
 JAMES B. SMITH, JR.

 ? "SELLING PRICE IS "
 SELLING PRICE IS   500

 ? TEXAS
 TEXAS

 ** DONE **
```

```
>NEW

>100 INPUT I,A(I)
>110 PRINT I:A(3)
>120 END
 RUN
 ? 3,7
  3
  7

 ** DONE **
```

INPUT

When input information is entered, it is validated by the computer. If the input data is invalid, the message "WARNING: INPUT ERROR, TRY AGAIN" appears on the screen and you must reenter the line. Here are some causes of this message:

- if you try to enter input data that contains more or fewer values than requested by the INPUT statement.
- if you try to enter a string constant when a number is required. (Remember, a number is a valid string, so you may enter a number when a string constant is required.)

If a number is input that causes an overflow, the message "WARNING: NUMBER TOO BIG, TRY AGAIN" appears on the screen and you must reenter the line. If a number is input that causes an underflow, the value is replaced by zero. No warning message is given.

Examples:

```
>NEW

>100 INPUT A,B$
>110 PRINT A;B$
>120 END
>RUN
 ? 12,HI,3

 * WARNING:
    INPUT ERROR IN 100
 TRY AGAIN: HI,3

 * WARNING:
    INPUT ERROR IN 100
 TRY AGAIN: 23,HI
  23 HI

 ** DONE **
```

```
>NEW

>100 INPUT A
>110 PRINT A
>120 END
>RUN
 ? 23E139

 * WARNING:
    NUMBER TOO BIG IN 100
 TRY AGAIN: 23E-139
 0

 ** DONE **
```

READ

READ *variable-list*

The READ statement allows you to read data stored inside your program in DATA statements. The *variable-list* specifies those variables that are to have values assigned. Variable names in the *variable-list* are separated by commas. The *variable-list* may include numeric variables and/or string variables.

The computer reads each DATA statement sequentially from left to right and assigns values to the variables in the *variable-list* from left to right. Subscript expressions in the *variable-list* are not evaluated until variables to the left have been assigned.

DATA statements are normally read in line-number order. Each time a READ statement is performed, values for the variables in the *variable-list* are assigned sequentially, using all the items in the data-list of the current DATA statement before moving to the next DATA statement. You can override this sequencing, however, by using the RESTORE statement.

By following the program on the right, you can see how the READ, DATA, and RESTORE statements interact. In line 120 the computer begins assigning values to A and B from the DATA statement with the lowest line number, line 180. The first READ, therefore, assigns $A = 2$ and $B = 4$. The next performance of the READ statement still takes data from line 180 and assigns $A = 6$, $B = 8$. The third READ assigns the last item in line 180 to the variable A and the first item in line 190 to the variable B, so $A = 10$, $B = 12$. The fourth READ, the last in the J-loop, continues to get data from line 190, so $A = 14$, $B = 16$. Before going through the I-loop again, however, note that the computer encounters a RESTORE statement in line 160 which directs it to get data from the beginning of line 190 for the next READ statement. The computer then completes the program by reading the data from line 190 and then from line 200.

Examples:

```
>NEW

>100 FOR I=1 TO 3
>110 READ X,Y
>120 PRINT X;Y
>130 NEXT I
>140 DATA 22,15,36,52,48,96.5

>150 END
>RUN
   22    15
   36    52
   48    96.5

 ** DONE **
```

```
>NEW

>100 READ I,A(I)
>110 DATA 2,35
>120 PRINT A(2)
>130 END
>RUN
   35

 ** DONE **
```

```
>NEW

>100 FOR I=1 TO 2
>110 FOR J=1 TO 4
>120 READ A,B
>130 PRINT A;B;
>140 NEXT J
>150 PRINT
>160 RESTORE 190
>170 NEXT I
>180 DATA 2,4,6,8,10
>190 DATA 12,14,16,18
>200 DATA 20,22,24,26
>210 END
>RUN
   2   4   6   8   10   12   14   16
   12  14  16  18  20   22   24
   26

 ** DONE **
```

READ

When data is read from a DATA statement, the type of data in the data-list and the type of variables to which the values are assigned must correspond. If you try to assign a string value to a numeric variable, the message "DATA ERROR IN xx" (xx is the line number of the READ statement where the error occurs) appears on the screen and the program stops running. Remember that a number is a valid string so numbers may be assigned to either string or numeric variables.

When a READ statement is performed, if there are more names in the *variable-list* than values remaining in DATA statements, a "DATA ERROR" message is displayed on the screen and the program stops running. If a numeric constant is read which causes an underflow, its value is replaced by zero — no warning is given — and the program continues running normally. If a numeric constant is read which causes an overflow, its value is replaced by the appropriate computer limit, the message "WARNING: NUMBER TOO BIG" is displayed on the screen, and the program continues. For information on underflow, overflow, and numeric limits, see "Numeric Constants."

Examples:

```
>NEW

>100 READ A,B
>110 DATA 12,HELLO
>120 PRINT A;B
>130 END
>RUN

  * DATA ERROR IN 100

>■
```

```
>NEW

>100 READ A,B
>110 DATA 12E-135
>120 DATA 36E142
>130 PRINT :A:B
>140 READ C
>150 END
>RUN

  * WARNING:
    NUMBER TOO BIG IN 100

  0
  9.99999E+**

  * DATA ERROR IN 140

>■
```

DATA

DATA *data-list*

The DATA statement allows you to store data inside your program. Data in the *data-lists* are obtained via READ statements when the program is run. The *data-list* contains the values to be assigned to the variables specified in the variable-list of a READ statement. Items in the *data-list* are separated by commas. When a program reaches a DATA statement, it proceeds to the next statement with no other effect.

DATA statements may appear anywhere in a program, but the order in which they appear is important. Data from the *data-lists* are read sequentially, beginning with the first item in the first DATA statement. If your program includes more than one DATA statement, the DATA statements are read in ascending line-number order unless otherwise specified by a RESTORE statement. Thus, the order in which the data appears within the *data-list* and the order of the DATA statements within the program normally determine in which order the data is read.

Data in the *data-list* must correspond to the type of the variable to which it is assigned. Thus, if a numeric variable is specified in the READ statement, a numeric constant must be in the corresponding place in the DATA statement. Similarly, if a string variable is specified, a string constant must be in the corresponding place in the DATA statement. Remember that a number is a valid string, so you may have a number in the corresponding place in the DATA statement when a string constant is required.

When using string constants in a DATA statement, you may enclose the string in quotes. However, if the string you include contains a comma, a leading quote mark, leading spaces, or trailing spaces, it *must* be enclosed in quotes.

If the list of string constants in the DATA statement contains adjacent commas, the computer assumes you want to enter a null string (a string with no characters). In the example on the right, the DATA statement in line 110 contains two adjacent commas. Thus, a null string is assigned to B$, as you can see when the program is run.

Examples:

```
>NEW

>100 FOR I=1 TO 5
>110 READ A,B
>120 PRINT A;B
>130 NEXT I
>140 DATA 2,4,6,7,8
>150 DATA 1,2,3,4,5
>160 END
>RUN
  2  4
  6  7
  8  1
  2  3
  4  5

** DONE **


>NEW

>100 READ A$,B$,C,D
>110 PRINT A$:B$:C:D
>120 DATA HELLO,"JONES, MARY"
,28,3.1416
>130 END
>RUN
 HELLO
 JONES, MARY
  28
  3.1416

** DONE **


>NEW

>100 READ A$,B$,C
>110 DATA HI,,2
>120 PRINT "A$ IS ";A$
>130 PRINT "B$ IS ";B$
>140 PRINT "C IS ";C
>150 END
 RUN
 A$ IS HI
 B$ IS
 C IS  2

** DONE **
```

RESTORE

RESTORE [line-number]

(See the "File Processing" section for information about using RESTORE in file processing.)

This form of the RESTORE statement tells your program which DATA statement to use with the next READ statement.

When RESTORE is used with no line-number and the next READ statement is performed, values will be assigned beginning with the first DATA statement in the program.

When RESTORE is followed by the line-number of a DATA statement and the next READ statement is performed, values will be assigned beginning with the first data-item in the DATA statement specified by the line-number.

If the line-number specified in a RESTORE statement is not a DATA statement or is not a program line number, then the next READ statement performed will start at the first DATA statement whose line number is greater than the one specified. If there is no DATA statement with a line number greater than or equal to the one specified, then the next READ statement performed will cause an out-of-data condition and a "DATA ERROR" message will be displayed. If the line-number specified is greater than the highest line number in the program, the program will stop running and the message "DATA ERROR IN xx" will be displayed.

Examples:

```
>NEW

>100 FOR I=1 TO 2
>110 FOR J=1 TO 4
>120 READ A
>130 PRINT A;
>140 NEXT J
>150 RESTORE 180
>160 NEXT I
>170 DATA 12,33,41,26,42,50
>180 DATA 10,20,30,40,50
>190 END
>RUN
   12  33  41  26  10  20  30
   40
  ** DONE **
```

```
>NEW

>100 FOR I=1 TO 5
>110 READ X
>120 RESTORE
>130 PRINT X;
>140 NEXT I
>150 DATA 10,20,30
>160 END
>RUN
   10  10  10  10  10
  ** DONE **
```

```
>NEW

>100 READ A,B
>110 RESTORE 130
>120 PRINT A;B
>130 READ C,D
>140 PRINT C;D
>150 DATA 26.9,34.67
>160 END
>RUN
   26.9  34.67
   26.9  34.67

  ** DONE **

>110 RESTORE 145
>RUN
   26.9  34.67
   26.9  34.67

  ** DONE **

>110 RESTORE 155
>RUN
   26.9  34.67

  * DATA ERROR IN 130

>■
```

PRINT

PRINT [*print-list*]

(For information on using the PRINT statement with files, see the "File Processing" section.)

The PRINT statement lets you print numbers and strings on the screen. The *print-list* consists of

- *print-items* — numeric expressions and string expressions which print on the screen and *tab-functions* which control print positioning (similar to the TAB key on the typewriter).
- *print-separators* — the punctuation between *print-items* (commas, colons, and semicolons) which serves as indicators for positioning data on the print-line.

When the computer performs a PRINT statement, the values of the expressions in the *print-list* are displayed on the screen in order from left to right, as specified by the *print-separators* and *tab-functions*.

Printing Strings

String expressions in the *print-list* are evaluated to produce a string result. There are no blank spaces inserted before or after a string. If you wish to print a blank space before or after a string, you can include it in the string or insert it separately with quotes.

Printing Numbers

Numeric expressions in the *print-list* are evaluated to produce a numeric result to be printed. Positive numbers are printed with a leading space (instead of a plus sign) and negative numbers are printed with a leading minus sign. All numbers are printed with a trailing space.

Examples:

```
>NEW

>100 A=10
>110 B=20
>120 STRING$="TI COMPUTER"
>130 PRINT A;B:STRING$
>140 PRINT "HELLO, FRIEND"
>150 END
>RUN
  10  20
 TI COMPUTER
 HELLO, FRIEND

 ** DONE **
```

```
>NEW

>100 N$="JOAN"
>110 M$="HI"
>120 PRINT M$;N$
>130 PRINT M$&" "&N$
>140 PRINT "HELLO ";N$
>150 END
>RUN
 HIJOAN
 HI JOAN
 HELLO JOAN

 ** DONE **
```

```
>NEW

>100 LET A=10.2
>110 B=-30.5
>120 C=16.7
>130 PRINT A;B;C
>140 PRINT A+B
>150 END
>RUN
  10.2 -30.5  16.7
-20.3

 ** DONE **
```

PRINT

The PRINT statement displays numbers in either *normal decimal form* or *scientific notation*, according to these rules:

1. All numbers with 10 or fewer digits are printed in *normal decimal form.*

2. Integer numbers with more than 10 digits are printed in *scientific notation.*

3. Non-integer numbers with more than 10 digits are printed in *scientific notation* only if they can be presented with more significant digits in *scientific notation* than in *normal decimal form.* If printed in *normal decimal form*, all digits beyond the tenth digit are omitted.

   If numbers are printed in *normal decimal form*, the following conventions are observed:

   ■ Integers are printed with no decimal point.

   ■ Non-integers have the decimal point printed in its proper place. Trailing zeros in the fractional part are omitted. If the number has more than ten digits, the tenth digit is rounded.

   ■ Numbers with a value less than one are printed with *no* digits to the left of the decimal point.

If numbers are printed in *scientific notation*, the format is:

> mantissa E exponent

and the following rules apply:

   ■ The mantissa is printed with 6 or fewer digits and is always displayed with one digit to the left of the decimal point.

   ■ Trailing zeros are omitted in the fractional part of the mantissa.

   ■ If there are more than five digits in the fractional part of the mantissa, the fifth digit is rounded.

   ■ The exponent is displayed with a plus or minus sign followed by a two-digit number.

   ■ If you attempt to print a number with an exponent value larger than +99 or smaller than −99, the computer will print ** following the proper sign of the exponent.

   ■ "E" must be an upper-case character.

Examples:

```
>PRINT -10;7.1
 -10  7.1


>PRINT 93427685127
 9.34277E+10


>PRINT 1E-10
 .0000000001

>PRINT 1.2E-10
 1.2E-10

>PRINT .000000000246
 2.46E-10


>PRINT 15;-3
 15 -3


>PRINT 3.350;-46.1
 3.35 -46.1

>PRINT 791.123456789
 791.1234568


>PRINT -12.7E-3;0.64
 -.0127  .64
```

```
>PRINT .0000000001978531
 1.97853E-10

>PRINT -98.77E21
 -9.877E+22

>PRINT 736.400E10
 7.364E+12

>PRINT 12.36587E-15
 1.23659E-14

>PRINT 1.25E-9;-43.6E12
 1.25E-09 -4.36E+13

>PRINT .76E126;81E-115
 7.6E+**  8.1E-**
```

PRINT

Print-Separators

Each screen line used with the PRINT statement has 28 character positions numbered from left to right (1-28). Each line is divided into two 14-character print zones. By using the *print-separators* and the *tab-function,* you can control the position of the *print-items* displayed on the screen.

There are three types of *print-separators:* semicolons, colons, and commas. At least one *print-separator* must be placed between adjacent *print-items* in the *print-list.* Multiple *print-separators* may be used side by side and are evaluated from left to right.

The *semicolon print-separator* causes adjacent *print-items* to print side by side with no extra spaces between the values. In the program on the right, the spaces after the numbers appear only because all numbers are printed with a trailing space regardless of the type of *print-separator* used.

The *colon print-separator* causes the next *print-item* to print at the beginning of the next line.

Print lines are divided into two zones. The first zone begins in column 1 and the second begins in column 15. When the computer evaluates a *comma print-separator,* the next *print-item* is printed at the beginning of the next zone. If it is already in the second print zone when a *comma print-separator* is evaluated, the next *print-item* is begun on the next line.

Examples:

```
>PRINT "A"::"B"
 A

 B


>NEW

>100 A=-26
>110 B=-33
>120 C$="HELLO"
>130 D$="HOW ARE YOU?"
>140 PRINT A;B;C$;D$
>150 END
>RUN
 -26 -33 HELLOHOW ARE YOU?

** DONE **


>NEW

>100 A=-26
>110 B$="HELLO"
>120 C$="HOW ARE YOU?"
>130 PRINT A:B$:C$
>140 END
>RUN
 -26
 HELLO
 HOW ARE YOU?

** DONE **


>NEW

>100 A$="ZONE 1"
>110 B$="ZONE 2"
>120 PRINT A$,B$
>130 PRINT A$:,B$,A$
>140 END
>RUN
 ZONE 1        ZONE 2
 ZONE 1
               ZONE 2
 ZONE 1

** DONE **
```

PRINT

Tab-Function

The *tab-function* specifies the starting position on the print-line for the next *print-item*. The format of the *tab-function* is:

TAB *(numeric-expression)*

The numeric-expression is evaluated and rounded to the nearest integer *n*. If *n* is less than one, then its value is replaced by one. If *n* is greater than 28, then *n* is repeatedly reduced by 28 until $1 \leq n \leq 28$. If the number of characters already printed on the current line is less than or equal to *n*, the next *print-item* is printed beginning in position *n*. If the number of characters already printed on the current line is greater than *n*, then the next item is printed on the next line beginning in position *n*. Note that the *tab-function* is a *print-item* and thus must be preceded by a *print-separator*, except when it is the first item in the *print-list*. The *tab-function* must also be followed by a *print-separator*, except when it is the last item in the *print-list*. The *print-separator* before a *tab-function* is evaluated before the *tab-function*, and the *print-separator* following the *tab-function* is evaluated after the *tab-function*. Thus, you should use a *semicolon print-separator* before and after the *tab-function* for best results.

In the program on the right, the computer does the following:

- line 120 — prints A, moves to position 15, prints B
- line 130 — prints A, moves to the next print zone (in this case, position 15 of the current screen line), prints B
- line 140 — prints A, moves to position 15 as specified in the *tab-function*, moves to the next print zone because of the comma (in this case position 1 of the next screen line), prints B
- line 150 — moves to position 5, prints A, moves to position 6 of the next line (since position 6 of the current line was already past when A was printed), prints B
- line 160 — prints A, subtracts 28 from 43 to begin the *tab-function* within the allowable character positions, moves to position 15 (43−28=15), prints B

Examples:

```
>NEW

>100 A=23.5
>110 B=48.6
>120 MSG$="HELLO"
>130 REM N>28
>140 PRINT TAB(5);MSG$;TAB(33
);MSG$
>150 REM CHARACTERS ALREADY
PRINTED<=N
>160 PRINT A;TAB(10);B
>170 REM CHARACTERS ALREADY
PRINTED>N
>180 PRINT TAB(3);A;TAB(3);B
>190 END
>RUN
    HELLO
    HELLO
   23.5        48.6
    23.5
    48.6

** DONE **
```

```
>NEW

>100 A=326
>110 B=79
>120 PRINT A;TAB(15);B
>130 PRINT A,B
>140 PRINT A;TAB(15),B
>150 PRINT TAB(5);A;TAB(6);B
>160 PRINT A;TAB(43);B
>170 END
 RUN
  326            79
  326            79
  326
  79
      326
       79
  326            79

** DONE **
```

PRINT

A *print-item* will not be split between two screen lines unless the *print-item* is a string with more than twenty-eight characters. In that case the string is always begun on a new line and is printed with twenty-eight characters per line until the entire string is printed. If a numeric *print-item* is such that the only character not able to fit on the current line is a trailing space, then the number will be printed on the current line. If the number itself will not fit on the current line, it is printed on the next line.

The *print-list* may end with a *print-separator*. If the *print-list* is not terminated by a *print-separator* (line 130), the computer considers the current line completed when all the characters produced from the *print-list* are printed. In this case the first *print-item* in the next PRINT statement (line 140) always begins on a new line.

If the *print-list* ends with a *print-separator* (line 140), then the *print-separator* is evaluated and the first *print-item* in the next PRINT statement (line 160) will start in the position indicated by the *print-separator*.

You may use a PRINT statement with no *print-list*. When such a PRINT statement is performed, the computer advances to the first character position of the next screen line. This has the effect of skipping a line if the preceding PRINT statement has no *print-separator* at the end.

```
>NEW

>100 A=23767
>110 B=79856
>120 C=A+B
>130 D=B-A
>140 PRINT A;B;C;D
>150 PRINT "A=";A;"B=";B;"C="
;C;"D=";D
>160 END
>RUN
  23767  79856  103623  56089
 A= 23767 B= 79856 C= 103623
 D= 56089

 ** DONE **

>NEW

>100 A=23
>110 B=597
>120 PRINT A,
>130 PRINT B
>140 PRINT A;B;
>150 C=468
>160 PRINT C
>170 END
>RUN
  23              597
  23  597  468

 ** DONE **

>NEW

>100 A=20
>110 PRINT A
>120 PRINT
>130 B=15
>140 PRINT B
>150 END
>RUN
  20

  15

 ** DONE **

>NEW

>100 FOR J=1 TO 2
>110 FOR I=1 TO 3
>120 PRINT I;
>130 NEXT I
>140 PRINT
>150 NEXT J
>160 END
>RUN
  1  2  3
  1  2  3

 ** DONE **
```

DISPLAY

DISPLAY [*print-list*]

The DISPLAY statement is identical to the PRINT statement when you use it to print items on the screen. The DISPLAY statement may not be used to write on any device except the screen. For a complete discussion of how to use this statement, follow the instructions for the PRINT statement.

```
>NEW

>100 A=35.6
>110 B$="HI!!"
>120 C=49.7
>130 PRINT B$:A;C
>140 DISPLAY B$:A;C
>150 END
>RUN
 HI!!
   35.6   49.7
 HI!!
   35.6   49.7

** DONE **
```

Color Graphics and Sound

Introduction

A special set of subprograms has been built into the TI computer to provide color graphics, sound, and other capabilities not usually found in BASIC.

Whenever you want to use one of these special subprograms, you *call* for it by name and supply a few specifications. The subprogram then takes over, performs its task, and provides you with such things as musical tones, screen colors, and special graphics characters. These features are particularly useful when you are programming simulations, graphs, patterns on the screen, or your own "computer music." All of the subprograms may be used in Command Mode as well as in programs.

The built-in subprograms can be grouped according to their function:

- INPUT subprograms — GCHAR, JOYST, KEY
- OUTPUT subprograms — CLEAR, HCHAR, VCHAR, SOUND, SCREEN
- INTERNAL subprograms — CHAR, COLOR (the results of these subprograms aren't evident until you use an OUTPUT operation to see the results on the screen).

The graphics subprograms feature a 24-row by 32-column screen display. The 28 print positions normally used in TI BASIC correspond to columns 3 through 30, inclusive, in the graphics subprograms. Because some display screens may not show the two leftmost and two rightmost characters, your graphics may be more satisfactory if you use columns 3 through 30 and ignore columns 1 and 2 on the left and 31 and 32 on the right. Experiment with different line lengths to determine how many positions show on your screen.

CLEAR subprogram

CALL CLEAR

The CLEAR subprogram is used to clear (erase) the entire screen.
When the CLEAR subprogram is called, the space character (code
32) is placed in all positions on the screen.

When the program on the right is run, the screen is cleared before
the PRINT statements are performed.

If the space character (code 32) has been redefined by the CALL
CHAR subprogram, the screen will be filled with the new
character, rather than with spaces, when CALL CLEAR is
performed.

Examples:

```
>PRINT "HELLO THERE!"
 HELLO THERE!
>CALL CLEAR

 --screen clears
```

```
>NEW

>100 CALL CLEAR
>110 PRINT "HELLO THERE!"
>120 PRINT "HOW ARE YOU?"
>130 END
>RUN

 --screen clears

 HELLO THERE!
 HOW ARE YOU?

 ** DONE **
```

```
>NEW

>100 CALL CHAR(32,"0103070F1F
 3F7FFF")
>110 CALL CLEAR
>120 GOTO 120
>RUN

 --screen will be filled
   with ◢
```

(Press **CLEAR** to stop
the program)

COLOR subprogram

CALL COLOR (character-set-number,foreground-color-code,background-color-code)

The COLOR subprogram provides a powerful design capability by allowing you to specify screen character colors. (To change the screen color itself, see the SCREEN subprogram.) The character-set-number, foreground-color-code, and background-color-code are numeric expressions.

Each character displayed on your computer screen has two colors. The color of the dots that make up the character itself is called the foreground color. The color that occupies the rest of the character position on the screen is called the background color. Sixteen colors are available on the TI computer, so your entries for foreground and background color must have a value of 1 through 16. The color codes are given in the table below:

Color Code	Color
1	Transparent
2	Black
3	Medium Green
4	Light Green
5	Dark Blue
6	Light Blue
7	Dark Red
8	Cyan
9	Medium Red
10	Light Red
11	Dark Yellow
12	Light Yellow
13	Dark Green
14	Magenta
15	Gray
16	White

If transparent (code 1) is specified, the present screen color shows through when a character is displayed. Until a CALL COLOR is performed, the standard foreground-color is black (code 2) and the standard background-color is transparent (code 1) for all characters. When a breakpoint occurs, all characters are reset to the standard colors.

Examples:

```
>NEW

>100 CALL CLEAR
>110 INPUT "FOREGROUND?":F
>120 INPUT "BACKGROUND?":B
>130 CALL CLEAR
>140 CALL COLOR(2,F,B)
>150 CALL HCHAR(12,3,42,28)
>160 GO TO 110
>RUN

  --screen clears

  FOREGROUND?2
  BACKGROUND?14

  --screen clears

  (28 black asterisks with
   a magenta background)
```

```
****************************

                    FOREGROUND?
```

(Press **CLEAR** to stop
the program)

```
>NEW

>100 CALL CLEAR
>110 CALL SCREEN(12)
>120 CALL COLOR(2,1,7)
>130 CALL HCHAR(12,3,42,28)
>140 GOTO 140
>RUN

  --screen clears

  (transparent asterisks with
   a dark-red background on a
   light-yellow screen)

****************************
```

(Press **CLEAR** to stop
the program)

COLOR subprogram

To use CALL COLOR you must also specify to which of sixteen character sets the character you are printing belongs. The list of ASCII character codes for the standard characters is given in the Appendix. The character is displayed in the color specified when you use CALL HCHAR or CALL VCHAR. The *character-set-numbers* are given below.

Set Number	Character Codes
1	32-39
2	40-47
3	48-55
4	56-63
5	64-71
6	72-79
7	80-87
8	88-95
9	96-103
10	104-111
11	112-119
12	120-127
13	128-135
14	136-143
15	144-151
16	152-159

Note that all 24 rows and 32 columns are filled with the space character until you place other characters in some of these positions. If you use character set 1 in the CALL COLOR statement, all space characters on the screen are changed to the *background-color* specified since the space character is contained in set 1. This change is demonstrated by the program on the right.

Examples:

```
>NEW

>100 CALL CLEAR
>110 CALL COLOR(1,16,14)
>120 CALL SCREEN(13)
>130 CALL VCHAR(1,15,35,24)
>140 GOTO 140
>RUN

  --screen clears

  --24 white #'s with
    a magenta background on a
    dark-green screen
```

```
                       #
                       #
                       #
                       #
                       #
                       #
                       #
                       #
                       #
                       #
                       #
```

  --Note that the screen color
    appears only at the top an
    bottom of the screen

(Press **CLEAR** to stop
the program)

SCREEN subprogram

CALL SCREEN *(color-code)*

The SCREEN subprogram enhances the graphic capabilities of the TI computer by allowing you to change the screen color. The standard screen color while a program is running is light green (*color-code* = 4).

The *color-code* is a numeric expression which, when evaluated, has a value of 1 through 16. The table of the sixteen available colors and their codes is given below.

Color-code	Color
1	Transparent
2	Black
3	Medium Green
4	Light Green
5	Dark Blue
6	Light Blue
7	Dark Red
8	Cyan
9	Medium Red
10	Light Red
11	Dark Yellow
12	Light Yellow
13	Dark Green
14	Magenta
15	Gray
16	White

When the CALL SCREEN is performed, the entire screen background changes to the color specified by the *color-code*. All characters on the screen remain the same unless you have specified a transparent foreground or background color for them. In that case, the screen color "shows through" the transparent foreground or background.

The screen is set to cyan (code 8) when a program stops for a breakpoint or terminates. If you CONTINUE a program after a breakpoint, the screen is reset to the standard color (light green).

Examples:

```
>NEW

>100 CALL CLEAR
>110 INPUT "SCREEN COLOR?":S
>120 INPUT "FOREGROUND?":F
>130 INPUT "BACKGROUND?":B
>140 CALL CLEAR
>150 CALL SCREEN(S)
>160 CALL COLOR(2,F,B)
>170 CALL HCHAR(12,3,42,28)
>180 GOTO 110
>RUN

--screen clears

SCREEN COLOR?7
FOREGROUND?13
BACKGROUND?16

--screen clears

--28 dark-green asterisks
  with a white background on
  a dark-red screen
```

```
****************************

SCREEN COLOR?
```

(Press **CLEAR** to stop the program)

CHAR subprogram

(Character definition)

CALL CHAR(*char-code,"pattern-identifier"*)

The CHAR subprogram allows you to define your own special graphics characters. You can redefine the standard set of characters (ASCII codes 32-127) and establish additional characters with codes 128-159.

The *char-code* specifies the code of the character you wish to define and must be a numeric expression with a value between 32 and 159, inclusive. If the character you are defining is in the range 128-159 and there is insufficient free memory to define the character, the program will terminate with a "MEMORY FULL" error.

The *pattern-identifier* is a 16-character string expression which specifies the pattern of the character you want to use in your program. This string expression is a coded representation of the 64 dots which make up a character position on the screen. These 64 dots comprise an 8-by-8 grid as shown below, greatly enlarged.

```
             LEFT    RIGHT
           BLOCKS | BLOCKS
ROW 1    ┌─┬─┬─┬─┬─┬─┬─┬─┐
ROW 2    ├─┼─┼─┼─┼─┼─┼─┼─┤
ROW 3    ├─┼─┼─┼─┼─┼─┼─┼─┤
ROW 4    ├─┼─┼─┼─┼─┼─┼─┼─┤
ROW 5    ├─┼─┼─┼─┼─┼─┼─┼─┤
ROW 6    ├─┼─┼─┼─┼─┼─┼─┼─┤
ROW 7    ├─┼─┼─┼─┼─┼─┼─┼─┤
ROW 8    └─┴─┴─┴─┴─┴─┴─┴─┘
```

Each row is partitioned into two blocks of four dots each:

```
ANY ROW   ┌─┬─┬─┬─┬─┬─┬─┬─┐
          └─┴─┴─┴─┴─┴─┴─┴─┘
          └───────┴───────┘
            LEFT    RIGHT
            BLOCK   BLOCK
```

Examples:

```
>NEW

>100 CALL CLEAR
>110 CALL CHAR(33,"FFFFFFFFFF
  FFFFFF")
>120 CALL COLOR(1,9,6)
>130 CALL VCHAR(12,16,33)
>140 GOTO 140
>RUN

  --screen clears
                ■
```

(Press **CLEAR** to stop the program)

CHAR subprogram

Each character in the string expression describes the pattern of dots in one block of a row. The rows are described from left to right and from top to bottom. That is, the first two characters in the string describe the pattern for row one of the dot-grid, the next two describe row two, and so on.

Characters are created by turning some dots "on" and leaving others "off." The space character (code 32) is a character with all the dots turned "off." Turning all the dots "on" produces a solid block (■).

All the standard characters are automatically set so that they turn "on" the appropriate dots. To create a new character, you must tell the computer what dots to turn on or leave off in each of the 16 blocks that contain the character. In the computer a binary code is used to specify what dots are on or off within a particular block. However, a "shorthand" method called hexadecimal, made up of numbers and letters, is used to control the on/off condition. The table that follows contains all the possible on/off conditions for the dots within a given block and the hexadecimal notation for each condition.

Blocks	Binary Code (0 = Off; 1 = On)	Hexadecimal Code
	0000	0
	0001	1
	0010	2
	0011	3
	0100	4
	0101	5
	0110	6
	0111	7
	1000	8
	1001	9
	1010	A
	1011	B
	1100	C
	1101	D
	1110	E
	1111	F

Note: The hexadecimal codes A, B, C, D, E and F must be entered from the keyboard as upper-case characters.

CHAR subprogram

To describe the dot pattern pictured below you would code this string for CALL CHAR:

"1898FF3D3C3CE404"

	LEFT BLOCKS	RIGHT BLOCKS	BLOCK CODES
ROW 1			18
ROW 2			98
ROW 3			FF
ROW 4			3D
ROW 5			3C
ROW 6			3C
ROW 7			E4
ROW 8			04

If the string expression is less than 16 characters, the computer will assume that the remaining characters are zero. If the string is longer than 16 characters, the computer will ignore the excess.

Remember that CALL CHAR only defines a character. To display the character on the screen you will need to use CALL HCHAR, CALL VCHAR, PRINT, or DISPLAY. When CALL CHAR is performed, any character already on the screen with the same *char-code* is changed to the new character.

CHAR subprogram

If a program stops for a breakpoint, those characters redefining codes 32-127 are reset to their normal representation. Those with codes 128-159 are unchanged. When the program ends either normally or because of an error, all redefined characters are reset and any characters assigned to codes 128-159 are reset to be undefined.

Examples:

```
> NEW

> 100 CALL CLEAR
> 110 CALL CHAR(128,"FFFFFFFF
  FFFFFF")
> 120 CALL CHAR(42,"0F0F0F0F0F
  0F0F0F")
> 130 CALL HCHAR(12,17,42)
> 140 CALL HCHAR(14,17,128)
> 150 FOR DELAY=1 to 350
> 160 NEXT DELAY
> 170 END
> RUN

  --screen clears
```

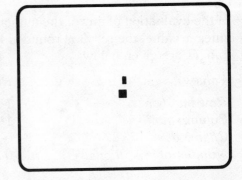

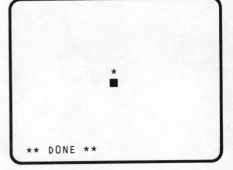

```
> CALL HCHAR(24,5,42)
      *
```

HCHAR subprogram
(Horizontal character repetition)

CALL HCHAR *(row-number, column-number, char-code [,number-of-repetitions])*

The HCHAR subprogram places a character anywhere on the screen and, optionally, repeats it horizontally. The *row-number* and *column-number* locate the starting position on the screen. The *row-number, column-number, char-code,* and *number-of-repetitions* are numeric expressions.

Examples:

```
>CALL CLEAR

--screen clears

>CALL HCHAR(10,1,72,50)
```

```
HHHHHHHHHHHHHHHHHHHHHHHHHHHHH
HHHHHHHHHHHHHHHHH




>CALL HCHAR(10,1,72,50)
```

If the evaluation of any of the numeric expressions results in a non-integer value, the result is rounded to obtain an integer. The valid ranges are given below:

Value	Range
Row-number	1-24, inclusive
Column-number	1-32, inclusive
Char-code	0-32767, inclusive
Number-of-repetitions	0-32767, inclusive

```
>NEW

>100 CALL CLEAR
>110 FOR S=2 TO 16
>120 CALL COLOR(S,S,S)
>130 NEXT S
>140 CHR=40
>150 FOR X=8 TO 22
>160 CALL VCHAR(4,X,CHR,15)
>170 CALL HCHAR(X-4,8,CHR,15)

>180 CHR=CHR+8
>190 NEXT X
>200 GOTO 140
>RUN

--screen clears

--makes a pattern on the
  screen using various COLOR
```

(Press **CLEAR** to stop
the program)

HCHAR subprogram

A value of 1 for *row-number* indicates the top of the screen. A value of 1 for *column-number* indicates the left side of the screen. The screen can be thought of as a "grid" as shown here.

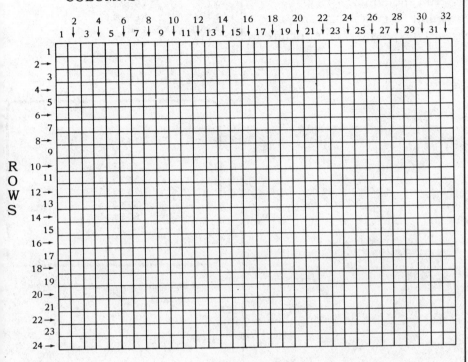

Because columns 1, 2, 31, and 32 may not show on your screen, you may want to use only *column-numbers* 3 through 30.

Although you may specify a value as large as 32767 for *char-code*, the computer will convert the value specified to a range of 0 through 255. Character codes 32 through 127 are defined as the standard ASCII character codes. Character codes 128 through 159 may be defined using the CHAR subprogram. If you specify an undefined character for *char-code*, you get whatever is in memory at the time the HCHAR subprogram is called.

```
>CALL HCHAR(24,14,29752)
         8
>CALL HCHAR(24,14,35)
         #
>CALL HCHAR(24,14,132)
 --displayed character depends
   on what is in memory now
```

HCHAR subprogram

To repeat the specified character, enter a value for the *number-of-repetitions*. The computer will display the character beginning at the specified starting position and continue on the left side of the next line. If the bottom of the screen is reached, the display will continue on the top line of the screen. You should use 768 for *number-of-repetitions* to fill all 24 rows and 32 columns. Using a number larger than 768 will unnecessarily extend the time required to perform this statement.

Examples:

```
>NEW

>100 CALL CLEAR
>110 FOR I=9 TO 15
>120 CALL HCHAR(I,13,36,6)
>130 NEXT I
>140 GOTO 140
>RUN

  --screen clears
```

```
        $$$$$$
        $$$$$$
        $$$$$$
        $$$$$$
        $$$$$$
        $$$$$$
        $$$$$$
```

(Press **CLEAR** to stop
the program)

VCHAR subprogram
(Vertical character repetition)

CALL VCHAR *(row-number, column-number, char-code* [*,number-of-repetitions*])

The VCHAR subprogram performs very much like the HCHAR subprogram except that it repeats characters vertically rather than horizontally. The computer will display the character beginning at the specified position and continuing down the screen. If the bottom of the screen is reached, the display will continue at the top of the next column to the right. If the right edge of the screen is reached, the display will continue at the left edge. See the HCHAR subprogram for more details.

Examples:
```
>CALL CLEAR

 --screen clears

>CALL VCHAR(2,10,86,13)
```

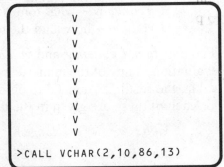

```
>NEW

>100 CALL CLEAR
>110 FOR I=13 TO 18
>120 CALL VCHAR(9,I,36,6)
>130 NEXT I
>140 GOTO 140
>RUN

 -- screen clears
```

```
        $$$$$$$
        $$$$$$$
        $$$$$$$
        $$$$$$$
        $$$$$$$
        $$$$$$$
```

(Press **CLEAR** to stop
the program)

SOUND subprogram

CALL SOUND(*duration,frequency1,volume1*[*,frequency2,volume2*][*,frequency3,volume3*][*,frequency4,volume*

The SOUND subprogram tells the computer to produce tones of different frequencies. The values you include control three aspects of the tone:

- *duration* — how long the tone lasts.
- *frequency* — what tone actually plays.
- *volume* — how loud the tone is.

The *duration, frequency,* and *volume* are numeric expressions. If the evaluation of any of the numeric expressions results in a non-integer value, the result is rounded to obtain an integer. The valid ranges for each of these are given in the table and discussed further below.

Value	Range
duration	1 to 4250, inclusive
	−1 to −4250, inclusive
frequency	(Tone) 110 to 44733, inclusive
	(Noise) −1 to −8, inclusive
volume	0 (loudest) to 30 (quietest), inclusive

Duration

The *duration* you specify is measured in milliseconds. One second is equal to 1000 milliseconds. Thus, the duration ranges from .001 to 4.25 seconds. (The actual duration may vary as much as 1/60th of a second.) The *duration* you specify applies to each sound generated by a particular CALL SOUND statement.

In a program, the computer continues performing program statements while a sound is being played. When you call the SOUND subprogram, the computer will wait until the previous sound has been completed before performing the new CALL SOUND statement unless a negative *duration* is specified. If you specify a negative *duration* in the new CALL SOUND statement, the previous sound is stopped and the new one is begun immediately.

Examples:

```
>CALL SOUND(100,294,2)

 --plays a single tone
```

```
>NEW

>100 TONE=110
>110 FOR COUNT=1 TO 10
>120 CALL SOUND(-500,TONE,1)
>130 TONE=TONE+110
>140 NEXT COUNT
>150 END
>RUN

 -- plays ten tones quickly

 ** DONE **

>120 CALL SOUND(+500,TONE,1)
>RUN

 --plays ten tones slowly

 ** DONE **
```

SOUND subprogram

Frequency

The *frequency* you specify may be either a tone or a noise. The tones, measured in Hertz (one cycle per second, [Hz]), can be specified from a low-pitch of 110 Hz to a high pitch of 44733 Hz, well above human hearing limits. (The actual frequency produced may vary from zero to ten percent depending on the *frequency.)* The frequencies for some common musical notes are given in the Appendix.

If a negative value for *frequency* is specified, a noise, rather than a tone, is produced. The noise is either "white noise" or "periodic noise." The noise associated with each value is given in the table below. Since it is difficult to describe the difference between noises, you can try out the different noises yourself to become familiar with each one.

Noise Characteristics

Frequency Value	Characteristic
−1	"Periodic Noise" Type 1
−2	"Periodic Noise" Type 2
−3	"Periodic Noise" Type 3
−4	"Periodic Noise" that varies with the frequency of the third tone specified
−5	"White Noise" Type 1
−6	"White Noise" Type 2
−7	"White Noise" Type 3
−8	"White Noise" that varies with the frequency of the third tone specified

A maximum of three tones and one noise can be activated simultaneously. For each tone or noise specified, its volume must be indicated immediately following the tone or noise.

Examples:

```
>CALL SOUND(1000,440,2)

 --plays a single tone

>CALL SOUND(500,-1,2)

 --plays a single noise


>NEW

>100 FOR NOISE=-1 TO -8 STEP
 -1
>110 CALL SOUND(1000,NOISE,2)

>120 NEXT NOISE
>130 END
>RUN

 --all 8 different noises
    are generated

** DONE **


>CALL SOUND(2000,-3,5)

 --plays a single noise




>CALL SOUND(2500,440,2,659,5,
880,10,-6,15)

 --plays 3 tones and 1 noise

>DUR=2500
>VOL=2
>C=262
>E=330
>G=392
>CALL SOUND(DUR,C,VOL,E,VOL,G
,VOL)

 --produces a C-major chord
```

GCHAR subprogram

(Get character)

CALL GCHAR *(row-number,column-number,numeric-variable)*

The GCHAR subprogram allows you to read a character from anywhere on the display screen. The position of the character you want is described by *row-number* and *column-number*. The computer puts the ASCII numeric code of the requested character into the *numeric-variable* you specify in the CALL GCHAR statement.

The *row-number* and *column-number* are numeric expressions. If the evaluation of the numeric expressions results in a non-integer value, the result is rounded to obtain an integer. A value of 1 for *row-number* indicates the top of the screen. A value of 1 for *column-number* specifies the left side of the screen. The screen can be thought of as a "grid" as shown here.

Examples:

```
>NEW

>100 CALL CLEAR
>110 CALL HCHAR(1,1,36,768)
>120 CALL GCHAR(5,10,X)
>130 CALL CLEAR
>140 PRINT X
>150 END
>RUN

 --screen clears

 --screen fills with $$$
   (code 36)

 --screen clears

 36

 ** DONE **
```

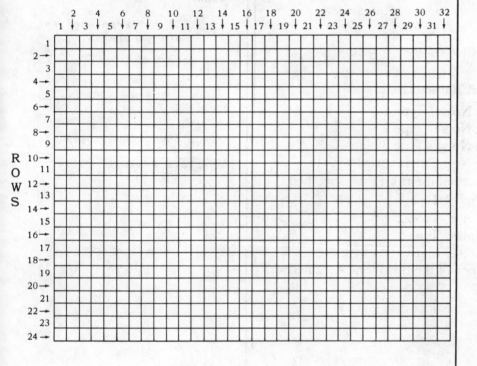

KEY subprogram

CALL KEY *(key-unit, return-variable, status-variable)*

The KEY subprogram allows you to transfer one character from the keyboard directly to your program. This eliminates the need for an INPUT statement and saves time in getting data from a single key into memory. Because the character represented by the key pressed is not displayed on the screen, the information already on the screen is not disturbed by performing the CALL KEY statement. The *key-unit,* which indicates which keyboard is the input device, is a numeric expression which, when evaluated, has a value 0 through 5, as shown below:

- 0 = console keyboard, in mode previously specified by CALL KEY
- 1 = left side of console keyboard or remote control 1
- 2 = right side of console keyboard or remote control 2
- 3, 4, 5 = specific modes for console keyboard

A *key-unit* of 0 remaps the keyboard in whatever mode was specified in the previous CALL KEY program line.

Key-units of 1 and 2 are used for a split-keyboard scan, when you want to separate the console keyboard into two smaller duplicate keyboards or when you are using the remote controller firebuttons as input devices.

Specifying 3, 4, or 5 as *key-unit* maps the keyboard to a particular mode of operation. The keyboard mode you specify determines the character codes returned by certain keys.

A *key-unit* of 3 places the computer in the standard TI-99/4 keyboard mode. (Most Command Module software uses this mode.) In this mode, both upper- and lower-case alphabetical characters are returned by the computer as upper-case only, and the function keys (**BACK,BEGIN,CLEAR,** etc.) return codes 1 through 15. No control characters are active.

A *key-unit* of 4 remaps the keyboard in the Pascal mode. Here, both upper- and lower-case alphabetical character codes are returned by the computer, and the function keys return codes ranging from 129 through 143. The control character codes are 1 through 31.

A *key-unit* of 5 places the keyboard in the BASIC mode. Both upper- and lower-case alphabetical character codes are returned by the computer. The function key codes are 1 through 15, and the control key codes are 128 through 159 (and 187).

KEY subprogram

The *return-variable* must be a numeric variable. The computer will place in *return-variable* the numeric character code represented by the key pressed. If the unit used is the console keyboard (unit 0), the character codes are the normal ASCII codes and may range from 0-127. If you are using the split keyboard (unit 1 and/or unit 2), the character codes will be 0 through 19.

The *status-variable* is a numeric variable which serves as an indicator to let you know what happened at the keyboard. The computer will return one of the following codes to the *status-variable* after performing the CALL KEY routine:

- **■** +1 = a new key was pressed since the last performance of the CALL KEY routine
- **■** −1 = the same key was pressed during the performance of CALL KEY as was pressed during the previous performance
- **■** 0 = no key was pressed

You can then check this status indicator in your program to determine what action to take next, as shown in line 110 of the program on the right. Line 110 is a test that gives you time to find and press a different key before the computer continues on to the next statement.

The following diagrams illustrate the control and function key codes returned in the various keyboard modes.

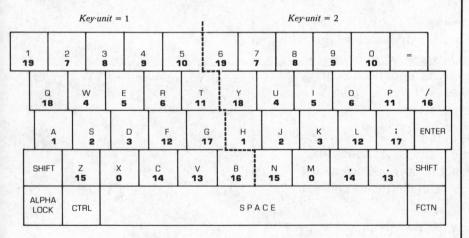

Figure 1. *Split Keyboard Scan.*
Codes returned = 0 through 19.

```
>NEW

>100 CALL KEY(0,KEY,STATUS)
>110 IF STATUS=0 THEN 100
>120 NOTE=KEY-64
>130 ON NOTE GOTO 250,270,150
 ,170,190,210,230
>140 GOTO 100
>150 NOTE=262
>160 GOTO 280
>170 NOTE=294
>180 GOTO 280
>190 NOTE=330
>200 GOTO 280
>210 NOTE=349
>220 GOTO 280
>230 NOTE=392
>240 GOTO 280
>250 NOTE=440
>260 GOTO 280
>270 NOTE=494
>280 CALL SOUND(100,NOTE,2)
>290 GOTO 100
>RUN

--plays a different note on
  the scale as you press
  the corresponding key (A-G)
```

(Press **CLEAR** to stop
the program)

3	4	7	2	14	12	1	6	15		5
1	2	3	4	5	6	7	8	9	0	=

Q	W	11 E	R	T	Y	U	I	O	P	/

A	8 S	9 D	F	G	H	J	K	L	;	13 ENTER

SHIFT	Z	10 X	C	V	B	N	M	,	.	SHIFT

ALPHA LOCK	CTRL	SPACE	FCTN

Figure 2. *Standard TI-99/4 Keyboard Scan.*
Key-unit = 3. Both upper- and lower-case
alphabetical characters returned as upper-case.
Function codes = 1 through 15.
No control characters active.

131	132	135	130	142	140	129	134	143		133
1	2	3	4	5	6	7	8 30	9 31	0	= 29

Q 17	W 23	139 E 5	R 18	T 20	Y 25	U 21	I 9	O 15	P 16	/

A 1	136 S 19	137 D 4	F 6	G 7	H 8	J 10	K 11	L 12	; 28	141 ENTER

SHIFT	Z 26	138 X 24	C 3	V 22	B 2	N 14	M 13	,	. 27	SHIFT*

ALPHA LOCK	CTRL	SPACE	FCTN

Figure 3. *Pascal Keyboard Scan.*
Key-unit = 4. Upper- and lower-case characters active.
Function codes = 129 through 143.
Control character codes = 1 through 31.

3	4	7	2	14	12	1	6	15		5
1	2	3	4	5	6	7	8 158	9 159	0	= 157

Q 145	W 151	11 E 133	R 146	T 148	Y 153	U 149	I 137	O 143	P 144	/ 187

A 129	8 S 147	9 D 132	F 134	G 135	H 136	J 138	K 139	L 140	; 156	13 ENTER

SHIFT	Z 154	10 X 152	C 131	V 150	B 130	N 142	M 141	, 128	. 155	SHIFT

ALPHA LOCK	CTRL	SPACE	FCTN

Figure 4. *BASIC Keyboard Scan.*
Key-unit = 5. Upper- and lower-case characters active.
Function codes = 1 through 15.
Control character codes = 128 through 159, 187.

JOYST Subprogram

CALL JOYST *(key-unit,x-return,y-return)*

The JOYST subprogram allows you to input information to the computer based on the position of the lever on the Wired Remote Controllers accessory (available separately).

The *key-unit* is a numeric expression which, when evaluated, has a value of 1 through 4.

- 1 = controller 1
- 2 = controller 2
- 3, 4, and 5 = specific modes for console keyboard

Specifying a *key-unit* of 3, 4, or 5 maps the console keyboard to a particular mode of operation, as explained in the "KEY subprogram" section. If *key-unit* has a value of 3, 4, or 5, the computer will not properly detect input from the remote controllers.

Numeric variables must be used for *x-return* and *y-return*. The subprogram assigns an integer value of −4, +4, or 0 to each of these variables, based on the position of the joystick at that time, as shown below. The first value in parentheses is *x-return* and the second value is *y-return*.

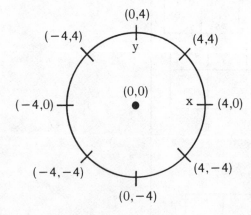

You may then use these values in your program by referring to the variable names.

You will find more detailed instructions in the manual enclosed with the optional remote controls.

```
>NEW

>100 CALL CLEAR
>110 CALL CHAR(42,"FFFFFFFFFF
 FFFFFF")
>120 INPUT "SCREEN COLOR?":S
>130 INPUT "BLOCK COLOR?":F
>140 CALL CLEAR
>150 CALL SCREEN(S)
>160 CALL COLOR(2,F,1)
>170 CALL JOYST(2,X,Y)
>180 A=X*2.2+16.6
>190 B=Y*1.6+12.2
>200 CALL HCHAR(B,A,42)
>210 GOTO 170
>RUN

  --screen clears

  SCREEN COLOR?14
  BLOCK COLOR?9

  --screen clears

--color block will move
  around screen as joystick
  controller is moved
```

(Press **CLEAR** to stop the program)

Built-In Numeric Functions

Introduction

Many special-purpose functions are built into TI BASIC. The functions described in this section perform some of the frequently used arithmetic operations. Obtaining the equivalent results for these functions requires a lot of programming in BASIC. Thus, they have been built in to TI BASIC and made easy for you to use. Built-in functions which are used with strings are discussed in the "Built-In String Functions" section. In addition to the built-in functions, you can also define your own functions (see "User-Defined Functions.")

ABS — Absolute Value

ABS*(numeric-expression)*

The absolute value function gives you the absolute value of the argument. The argument is the value obtained when the *numeric-expression* is evaluated. The normal rules for evaluating numeric expressions (see "Numeric Expressions") are used here. If the argument is positive, then the absolute value function gives you the argument itself. If the argument is negative, the absolute value function gives you the negative of the argument. Thus, for an argument, X:

- If $X \geq 0$, ABS(X) = X
- If $X < 0$, ABS(X) = -X
  (e.g., ABS(-3) = -(-3) = 3)

Examples:

```
>NEW

>100 A=-27.36
>110 B=9.7
>120 PRINT ABS(A);ABS(B)
>130 PRINT ABS(3.8);ABS(-4.5)

>140 PRINT ABS(-3*2)
>150 PRINT ABS(A*(B-3.2))
>160 END
>RUN
  27.36  9.7
  3.8  4.5
  6
  177.84

** DONE **
```

ATN — Arctangent

ATN*(numeric-expression)*

The arctangent function gives you the arctangent of the argument. The argument is the value obtained when the *numeric-expression* is evaluated. The normal rules for evaluating numeric expressions are used here. Thus, ATN(x) gives you the angle (in radians) whose tangent is x. If you want to get the equivalent angle in degrees, you need to multiply the answer you get by (180/4*ATN(1))) or 57.295779513079 which is $180/\pi$. The value given for the arctangent function is always in the range $-\pi/2 < \text{ATN(x)} < \pi/2$.

```
>NEW

>100 PRINT ATN(.44)
>110 PRINT ATN(1E127)
>120 PRINT ATN(1E-129);ATN(0)

>130 PRINT ATN(.3)*57.2957795
 13079
>140 PRINT ATN(.3)*(180/(4*AT
 N(1)))
>150 END
>RUN
  .4145068746
  1.570796327
  0  0
  16.69924423
  16.69924423

** DONE **
```

COS — Cosine

COS(*numeric-expression*)

The cosine function gives you the cosine of the argument, x, where x is an angle in radians. The argument is the value obtained when the *numeric-expression* is evaluated. The normal rules for evaluating numeric expressions are used here. If the angle is in degrees, multiply the degrees by $\pi/180$ to get the equivalent angle in radians. You may use $(4*ATN(1))/180$ or 0.01745329251994 for $\pi/180$. Note that if you enter a value of x where $|x| \geq 1.5707963266375*10^{10}$, the message "BAD ARGUMENT" is displayed and the program stops running.

Examples:

```
>NEW

>100  A=1.047197551196
>110  B=60
>120  C=.01745329251994
>130  PRINT COS(A);COS(B*C)
>140  PRINT COS(B*(4*ATN(1))/1
80)
>150  END
>RUN
   .5   .5
   .5

 ** DONE **

>PRINT COS(2.2E11)

  * BAD ARGUMENT
```

EXP — Exponential

EXP(*numeric-expression*)

The exponential function gives you the value of e^x, where $e = 2.718281828$. The argument, x, is the value obtained when the *numeric-expression* is evaluated. The normal rules for the evaluation of numeric expressions are used here. The exponential function is the inverse of the natural logarithm function (LOG). Thus, $X = EXP(LOG(X))$.

```
>NEW

>100  A=3.79
>110  PRINT EXP(A);EXP(9)
>120  PRINT EXP(A*2)
>130  PRINT EXP(LOG(2))
>140  END
>RUN
  44.25640028   8103.083928
  1958.628965
  2

 ** DONE **
```

INT — Integer

INT*(numeric-expression)*

The integer function gives you the largest integer that is not greater than the argument. The argument is the value obtained when the *numeric-expression* is evaluated. The normal rules for evaluating numeric expressions are used here. The integer function always gives you the closest integer which is to the left of the number specified on the number line. Thus, for positive numbers, the decimal portion is dropped; for negative numbers, the next smallest integer value is used (i.e., INT(-2.3) = -3). If you specify an integer, then the same integer is given.

Examples:

```
>NEW

>100 B=.678
>110 A=INT(B*100+.5)/100
>120 PRINT A;INT(B)
>130 PRINT INT(-2.3);INT(2.2)

>140 STOP
>RUN
  .68  0
 -3  2

** DONE **
```

LOG — Natural Logarithm

LOG*(numeric-expression)*

The natural logarithm function gives you the natural logarithm of the number specified by the argument. The argument is the value obtained when the *numeric-expression* is evaluated. The normal rules for the evaluation of numeric expressions are used here. The natural logarithm of x is usually shown as: $\log_e(x)$. The logarithm function is the inverse of the exponential function (EXP). Thus, $X = LOG(EXP(X))$.

The argument of the natural logarithm function must be greater than zero. If you specify a value for the argument which is less than or equal to zero, the message "BAD ARGUMENT" is displayed, and the program stops running.

If you want to find the logarithm of a number in another base, B, use this formula.

$$\log_B(X) = \log_e(X)/\log_e(B)$$

For example, $\log_{10}(3) = \log_e(3)/\log_e(10)$

```
>NEW

>100 A=3.5
>110 PRINT LOG(A);LOG(A*2)
>120 PRINT LOG(EXP(2))
>130 STOP
>RUN
  1.252762968  1.945910149
  2.

** DONE **


>PRINT LOG(-3)

 * BAD ARGUMENT


>PRINT LOG(3)/LOG(10)
  .4771212547
```

RANDOMIZE Statement

RANDOMIZE [seed]

The RANDOMIZE statement is used in conjunction with the random number function (RND). When the RANDOMIZE statement is not used, the random number function will generate the same sequence of pseudo-random numbers each time the program is run. When the RANDOMIZE statement is used without a seed, a different and unpredictable sequence of random numbers is generated by the random number function each time the program is run. If you use the RANDOMIZE statement with a seed specified, then the sequence of random numbers generated by the random number function depends upon the value of the seed. If the same seed is used each time the program is run, then the same sequence of numbers is generated. If a different seed is used each time the program is run, then a different sequence of numbers is generated. The seed may be any numeric expression. The number actually used for the seed is the first two bytes of the internal representation of the number. (See "Accuracy Information" in the Appendix for a complete explanation.) Thus, it is possible that the same sequence of numbers may be generated even if you specify different seeds. For example, RANDOMIZE 1000 and RANDOMIZE 1099 produce the same first two bytes internally and thus the same sequence of numbers. If the seed you specify is not an integer, then the value used is INT (seed) (see "INT-Integer").

Examples:

```
>NEW

>100 RANDOMIZE 23
>110 FOR I=1 TO 5
>120 PRINT INT(10*RND)+1
>130 NEXT I
>140 STOP
>RUN
  6
  4
  3
  8
  8

** DONE **
```

RND — Random Number

RND

The random number function gives you the next pseudo-random number in the current sequence of pseudo-random numbers. The random number generated will be greater than or equal to zero and less than one. The sequence of random numbers generated by the random number function is the same every time the program is run unless the RANDOMIZE statement appears in the program.

If you wish to obtain random integers between two values A and B (A<B), inclusive, use this formula:

$$INT((B-A+1)*RND)+A$$

```
>NEW

>100 FOR I=1 TO 5
>110 PRINT INT(10*RND)+1
>120 NEXT I
>130 END
>RUN
  6
  4
  6
  4
  3

 ** DONE **


>NEW

>100 REM RANDOM INTEGERS
  BETWEEN 1 AND 20,INCLUSIVE
>110 FOR I=1 TO 5
>120 C=INT(20*RND)+1
>130 PRINT C
>140 NEXT I
>150 END
>RUN
  11
  8
  11
  8
  6

 ** DONE **
```

SGN — Signum (Sign)

SGN*(numeric-expression)*

The signum function gives you the algebraic sign of the value specified by the argument. The argument is the value obtained when the *numeric-expression* is evaluated. The normal rules for the evaluation of numeric expressions are used here. The signum function gives different values depending on the value of the argument. These values are given here. For argument, X:

- $X < 0$, SGN(X) = −1
- $X = 0$, SGN(X) = 0
- $X > 0$, SGN(X) = 1

Examples:

```
>NEW

>100 A=-23.7
>110 B=6
>120 PRINT SGN(A);SGN(0);SGN(
 B)
>130 PRINT SGN(-3*3);SGN(B*2)

>140 END
>RUN
 -1  0  1
 -1  1

** DONE **
```

SIN — Sine

SIN*(numeric-expression)*

The sine function gives you the sine of the argument, x, where x is an angle in radians. The argument is the value obtained when the *numeric-expression* is evaluated. The normal rules for evaluating numeric expressions are used here. If the angle is in degrees, simply multiply the degrees by $\pi/180$ to get the equivalent angle in radians. You may use (4*ATN(1))/180 or 0.0174532925194 4 for $\pi/180$. Note that if you enter a value of x where $|x| \geq 1.5707963266375 * 10^{10}$, the message "BAD ARGUMENT" is displayed and the program stops running.

```
>NEW

>100 A=.5235987755982
>110 B=30
>120 C=.01745329251994
>130 PRINT SIN(A);SIN(B*C)
>140 PRINT SIN(B*(4*ATN(1))/1
 80)
>150 END
>RUN
 .5  .5
 .5

** DONE **


>PRINT SIN(1.9E12)

* BAD ARGUMENT
```

SQR — Square Root Function

SQR(*numeric-expression*)

The square root function gives you the positive square root of the value specified by the argument. The argument is the value obtained when the *numeric-expression* is evaluated. The normal rules for the evaluation of numeric expressions are used here. SQR(x) is equivalent to $x \wedge (1/2)$. The value specified by the argument may not be negative. If you specify a value for the argument which is less than zero, then the message "BAD ARGUMENT" is displayed and the program stops running.

Examples:

```
>NEW

>100 PRINT SQR(4);4∧(1/2)
>110 PRINT SQR(10)
>120 END
>RUN
  2  2
  3.16227766

** DONE **


>PRINT SQR(-5)

 * BAD ARGUMENT
```

TAN — Tangent

TAN(*numeric-expression*)

The tangent function gives you the tangent of the argument, x, where x is an angle in radians. The argument is the value obtained when the *numeric-expression* is evaluated. The normal rules for evaluating numeric expressions are used here. If the angle is in degrees, multiply the degrees by $\pi/180$ to get the equivalent angle in radians. You may use $(4*ATN(1))/180$ or 0.01745329251994 for $\pi/180$. Note that if you enter a value of x where $|x| \geq 1.5707963266375*10^{10}$, the message "BAD ARGUMENT" is displayed and the program stops running.

```
>NEW

>100 A=.7853981633973
>110 B=45
>120 C=.01745329251994
>130 PRINT TAN(A);TAN(B*C)
>140 PRINT TAN(B*(4*ATN(1))/1
 80)
>150 END
>RUN
  1.  1.
  1

** DONE **


>PRINT TAN(1.76E10)

 * BAD ARGUMENT
```

Built-In String Functions

Introduction

In addition to the built-in numeric functions, many other functions
are built into TI BASIC. The functions discussed in this section are
called string functions. String functions either use a string in some
way to produce a numeric result, or the result of the evaluation of
the function is a string. As you use your computer, you will find
many ways to use the string functions described here. You can also
define your own string functions (see "User-Defined Functions").
Note that any string function with a name that ends with a dollar
sign (e.g. CHR$) always gives a string result and cannot be used
in numeric expressions.

ASC — ASCII Value

ASC(*string-expression*)

The ASCII value function will give you the ASCII character code which corresponds to the first character of the string specified by the *string-expression*. A list of the ASCII character codes for each character in the standard character set is given in the Appendix.

Examples:

```
>NEW

>100 A$="HELLO"
>110 C$="JACK SPRAT"
>120 C=ASC(C$)
>130 B$="THE ASCII VALUE OF "

>140 PRINT B$;"H IS";ASC(A$)
>150 PRINT B$;"J IS";C
>160 PRINT B$;"N IS";ASC("NAM
 E")
>170 PRINT B$;"1 IS";ASC("1")

>180 PRINT CHR$(ASC(A$))
>190 END
>RUN
   THE ASCII VALUE OF H IS 72
   THE ASCII VALUE OF J IS 74
   THE ASCII VALUE OF N IS 78
   THE ASCII VALUE OF 1 IS 49
   H

 ** DONE **
```

CHR$ — Character

CHR$(*numeric-expression*)

The character function gives you the character corresponding to the ASCII character code specified in the argument. The argument is the value obtained when the *numeric-expression* is evaluated. The normal rules for the evaluation of numeric expressions are used here. If the argument specified is not an integer, it is rounded to obtain an integer. A list of the ASCII character codes for each character in the standard character set is given in the Appendix. If the argument specified is a value between 32 and 127, inclusive, a standard character is given. If the argument specified is between 128 and 159, inclusive, and a special graphics character has been defined for that value, the graphics character is given. If you specify an argument which designates an undefined character (i.e., not a standard character or a defined graphics character), then the character given is whatever is in memory at that time.

If you specify a value for the argument which is less than zero or greater than 32767, the message "BAD VALUE" is displayed, and the program stops running.

```
>NEW

>100 A$=CHR$(72)&CHR$(73)&CHR
 $(33)
>110 PRINT A$
>120 CALL CHAR(97,"0103070F1F
 3F7FFF")
>130 PRINT CHR$(32);CHR$(97)
>140 PRINT CHR$(3*14)
>150 PRINT CHR$(ASC("+"))
>160 END
>RUN
 HI!
 ◢
 *
 +

 ** DONE **




>PRINT CHR$(33010)

 * BAD VALUE
```

LEN — Length

LEN*(string-expression)*

The length function gives you the number of characters in the string specified by the argument. The argument is the string value obtained when the *string-expression* is evaluated. The normal rules for the evaluation of string expressions are used here. The length of a null string is zero. Remember that a space is a character and counts as part of the length.

Examples:

```
>NEW

>100 NAME$="CATHY"
>110 CITY$="NEW YORK"
>120 MSG$="HELLO "&"THERE!"
>130 PRINT NAME$;LEN(NAME$)
>140 PRINT CITY$;LEN(CITY$)
>150 PRINT MSG$;LEN(MSG$)
>160 PRINT LEN(NAME$&CITY$)
>170 PRINT LEN("HI!")
>180 STOP
>RUN
  CATHY  5
  NEW YORK  8
  HELLO THERE!  12
   13
   3

** DONE **
```

POS — Position

POS*(string-1,string-2,numeric-expression)*

The position function finds the first occurrence of *string-2* within *string-1*. Both *string-1* and *string-2* are string expressions. The *numeric-expression* is evaluated and rounded, if necessary, to obtain an integer, *n*. The normal rules for the evaluation of string expressions and numeric expressions are used here. The search for *string-2* begins at the *n*th character of *string-1*. If *string-2* is found, the character position within *string-1* of the first character of *string-2* is given. If *string-2* is not found, a value of zero is given. The position of the first character in *string-1* is position one. If you specify a value for *n* which is greater than the number of characters in *string-1*, a value of zero is given. If the value specified for *n* is less than zero, the message "BAD VALUE" is displayed and the program stops running.

```
>NEW

>100 MSG$="HELLO THERE! HOW A
RE YOU?"
>110 PRINT "H";POS(MSG$,"H",1
)
>120 C$="RE"
>130 PRINT C$;POS(MSG$,C$,1);
POS(MSG$,C$,12)
>140 PRINT "HI";POS(MSG$,"HI"
,1)
>150 END
>RUN
  H  1
  RE  10  19
  HI  0

** DONE **
```

SEG$ — String Segment

SEG$(string-expression,numeric-expression1,numeric-expression2)

The string segment function gives you a portion (substring) of the string designated by the *string-expression. Numeric-expression1* identifies the position of the character in the original string which is the first character of the substring. The position of the first character in the string specified is position one. The length of the substring is specified by *numeric-expression2.* The normal rules for the evaluation of numeric expressions and string expressions are used here.

For this discussion, A$ is used for *string-expression,* X is used for *numeric-expression1* and Y is used for *numeric-expression2.* If you specify a value for X which is greater than the length of A$ (line 110) or a value of zero for Y (line 120), then you are given the null string. If you specify a value for Y which is greater than the remaining length in A$ starting at the position specified by X (line 130), then you are given the rest of A$ starting at the position specified by X.

If you specify a value for X which is less than or equal to zero and/or specify a value for Y which is less than zero, then the message "BAD VALUE" is displayed and the program stops running.

Examples:

```
>NEW

>100 MSG$="HELLO THERE! HOW A
RE YOU?"
>110 REM SUBSTRING BEGINS IN
POSITION 14 AND HAS A LENGTH
OF 12.
>120 PRINT SEG$(MSG$,14,12)
>130 END
>RUN
HOW ARE YOU?

** DONE **
```

```
>NEW

>100 MSG$="I AM A COMPUTER."
>110 PRINT SEG$(MSG$,20,1)
>120 PRINT SEG$(MSG$,10,0)
>130 PRINT SEG$(MSG$,8,20)
>140 END
>RUN


COMPUTER.

** DONE **
```

```
>PRINT SEG$(MSG$,-1,10)

* BAD VALUE
```

STR$ — String-Number

STR$*(numeric-expression)*

The string-number function converts the number specified by the argument into a string. The argument is the value obtained when the *numeric-expression* is evaluated. The normal rules for the evaluation of numeric expressions are used here. When the number is converted into a string, the string is a valid representation of a numeric constant with no leading or trailing spaces. For example, if B = 69.5, then STR$ (B) is the string "69.5." Only string operations may be performed on the strings created using the string-number function. The string-number function is the inverse of the value function (VAL); see below. In the example, note that leading and trailing spaces are not present on the numbers converted to strings.

Examples:

```
>NEW

>100 A=-26.3
>110 PRINT STR$(A);" ";A
>120 PRINT 15.7;STR$(15.7)
>130 PRINT STR$(VAL("34.8"))
>140 END
>RUN
 -26.3 -26.3
  15.7 15.7
 34.8

 ** DONE **
```

VAL — Value

VAL*(string-expression)*

The value function is the inverse of the string-number function (STR$); see above. If the string specified by the *string-expression* is a valid representation of a numeric constant, then the value function converts the string to a numeric constant. For example, if A$ = "1234", then VAL(A$) = 1234. The normal rules for the evaluation of string expressions are used here. If the string specified is not a valid representation of a number or if the string is of zero length, the message "BAD ARGUMENT" is displayed and the program stops running. If you specify a string which is longer than 254 characters, the message "BAD ARGUMENT" is displayed and the program stops running.

```
>NEW

>100 P$="23.6"
>110 N$="-4.7"
>120 PRINT VAL(P$);VAL(N$)
>130 PRINT VAL("52"&".5")
>140 PRINT VAL(N$&"E"&"12")
>150 PRINT STR$(VAL(P$))
>160 END
>RUN
   23.6 -4.7
   52.5
  -4.7E+12
   23.6

 ** DONE **
```

User-Defined Functions

Introduction

In addition to the built-in functions described in the two previous sections, TI BASIC provides user-defined functions. User-defined functions can simplify programming by avoiding repeated use of complicated expressions. Once a function has been defined using the DEF statement, it may be used anywhere in the program by referencing the name you gave to the function.

DEFine

$$\text{DEF} \begin{Bmatrix} \textit{numeric-function-name } [(\textit{parameter})] = \textit{numeric-expression} \\ \textit{string-function-name } [(\textit{parameter})] = \textit{string-expression} \end{Bmatrix}$$

The DEFine statement allows you to define your own functions to use within a program. The *function-name* you specify may be any valid variable name. If you specify a *parameter* following the *function-name,* the *parameter* must be enclosed in parentheses and may be any valid variable name. Note that if the expression you specify evaluates to a string result, the *function-name* you use must be string variable name (i.e., the last character must be a dollar sign, $).

The DEFine statement specifies the function to be used based upon the *parameter* (if specified), variables, constants, and other built-in functions. Once a function has been defined, you may use the function in any string or numeric expression by entering the *function-name*. The *function-name* must be followed by an argument enclosed in parentheses if a *parameter* was specified in the DEF statement. If a function has no *parameter* specified, when a reference to the function is encountered in an expression, the function is evaluated using the current values of the variables which appear in the DEF statement.

If you specify a *parameter* for a function, when a reference to the function is encountered in an expression, the argument is evaluated and its value is assigned to the *parameter*. The expression in the DEF statement is then evaluated using the newly assigned value of the *parameter* and the current values of the other variables in the DEF statement.

Examples:

```
>NEW

>100 DEF PI=4*ATN(1)
>110 PRINT COS(60*PI/180)
>120 END
>RUN
  .5

  ** DONE **
```

```
>NEW

>100 REM EVALUATE Y=X*(X-3)
>110 DEF Y=X*(X-3)
>120 PRINT "  X   Y"
>130 FOR X=-2 TO 5
>140 PRINT X;Y
>150 NEXT X
>160 END
>RUN
   X   Y
  -2   10
  -1   4
   0   0
   1  -2
   2  -2
   3   0
   4   4
   5   10

  ** DONE **
```

```
>NEW

>100 REM TAKE A NAME AND
  PRINT IT BACKWARDS
>110 DEF BACK$(X)=SEG$(NAME$,
  X,1)
>120 INPUT "NAME? ":NAME$
>130 FOR I=LEN(NAME$) TO 1 ST
  EP -1
>140 BNAME$=BNAME$&BACK$(I)
>150 NEXT I
>160 PRINT NAME$:BNAME$
>170 END
>RUN
  NAME? ROBOT
  ROBOT
  TOBOR

  ** DONE **
```

DEF

The *parameter* used in the DEF statement is local to the DEF
statement in which it is used. This means that it is distinct from any
variable with the same name which is used in other statements in
the program. Thus, evaluating the function does not affect the value
of a variable which has the same name as the *parameter*.

A DEF statement is only performed when the function it defines is
referenced in an expression. When the computer encounters a DEF
statement while running a program, it takes no action but proceeds
to the next statement. A DEF statement may appear anywhere in a
program and need not logically precede a reference to the function,
but the function definition must have a lower line number than any
statement which references the function. A DEF statement can
reference other defined functions (line 170).

In a DEF statement, the function you specify may not reference
itself either directly (e.g. DEF B=B*2) or indirectly (e.g. DEF
F=G; DEF G = F). The *parameter* you specify may not be used as
an array. You can use an array element in a function definition as
long as the array does not have the same name as the *parameter*.

Examples:

```
>NEW

>100 DEF FUNC(A)=A*(A+B-5)
>110 A=6.9
>120 B=13
>130 PRINT "B= ";B:"FUNC(3)=
 ";FUNC(3):"A= ";A
>140 END
>RUN
 B=  13
 FUNC(3)=  33
 A=  6.9

** DONE **
```

```
>NEW

>100 REM FIND F'(X) USING
 NUMERICAL APPROXIMATION
>110 INPUT "X=? ":X
>120 IF ABS(X)>.01 THEN 150
>130 H=.00001
>140 GOTO 180
>150 H=.001*ABS(X)
>160 DEF F(Z)=3*Z^3-2*Z+1
>170 DEF DER(X)=(F(X+H)-F(X-H
 ))/(2*H)
>180 PRINT "F'(";STR$(X);")=
 ";DER(X)
>190 END
>RUN
 X=? .1
 F'(.1)= -1.90999997

** DONE **
```

```
>NEW

>100 DEF GX(X)=GX(2)*X
>110 PRINT GX(3)
>120 END
>RUN

* MEMORY FULL IN 110

>100 DEF GX(A)=A(3)^2
>RUN

* NAME CONFLICT IN 100
```

DEF

If you specify a *parameter* when defining a function, you must specify an argument when you reference the function. Similarly, if you do not specify a *parameter* when defining a function, you cannot specify an argument in the function reference.

Examples:

```
>NEW

>100 DEF SQUARE(X)=X*X
>110 PRINT SQUARE
>120 END
>RUN

 * NAME CONFLICT IN 110

>100 DEF PI=3.1416
>110 PRINT PI(2)
>RUN

 * NAME CONFLICT IN 110
```

Arrays

Introduction

An array is a collection of variables arranged in a way that allows you to use them easily in a computer program. The most common way of grouping variables is in a list, which is called a one-dimensional array. Each variable in the list is called an element of the array. The length of the list is limited only by the amount of memory available.

By using the array capability of TI BASIC you can do many things with a list — you can print the elements forward or backward, rearrange them, add them together, multiply them, or select certain ones for processing.

In TI BASIC an array may begin with element 0 or element 1. By using the OPTION BASE statement, you control which beginning element the computer establishes. For consistency in describing arrays, we are assuming that the first element in each array is element 1.

Let's say you want to use the computer to take two lists of four numbers and print all possible combinations of the numbers in both lists. You might call the first array X and the second one Y. Since X and Y name a *collection* of numbers, rather than a single variable, the computer needs a way to refer to the individual elements in each array. You must supply a pointer, called a subscript, to the particular element in the array you want the computer to use. This subscript is enclosed in parentheses and always immediately follows the name of the array. The subscript may be explicit, such as X(3), which refers to the third element in list X, or it may be a variable, as in X(T), where the value of T points to the proper element. In any case, the subscript is always either a positive integer or zero.

The program on the right pairs the numbers in array X and array Y. Notice that by using the array technique only a few program lines are needed for this relatively complex procedure.

Multi-Dimensional Arrays

With TI BASIC you can extend your use of arrays to include tabular information, arranged in rows and columns, called two-dimensional arrays. You can think of the TIC-TAC-TOE game as an example of a two-dimensional array.

X	O	X
O	X	X
X	O	O

Examples:

```
>NEW

>100 REM THIS PROGRAM PAIRS
 TWO LISTS
>110 REM LINES 120 TO 150
 ASSIGN VALUES TO LIST X
>120 FOR T=1 TO 4
>130 READ X(T)
>140 NEXT T
>150 DATA 1,3,5,7
>160 REM LINES 170 TO 200
 ASSIGN VALUES TO LIST Y
>170 FOR S=1 TO 4
>180 READ Y(S)
>190 NEXT S
>200 DATA 2,4,6,8
>210 REM LINES 220 TO 270
 PAIR THE LISTS AND PRINT
 THE COMBINATIONS
>220 FOR T=1 TO 4
>230 FOR S=1 TO 4
>240 PRINT X(T);Y(S);" ";
>250 NEXT S
>260 PRINT
>270 NEXT T
>280 END
>RUN
  1  2   1  4   1  6   1  8
  3  2   3  4   3  6   3  8
  5  2   5  4   5  6   5  8
  7  2   7  4   7  6   7  8

 ** DONE **
```

Arrays

You can represent the gameboard with this array:

T(1,1)	T(1,2)	T(1,3)
T(2,1)	T(2,2)	T(2,3)
T(3,1)	T(3,2)	T(3,3)

As in the one-dimensional arrays described earlier, you refer to a two-dimensional element with a subscript, in this case a double-subscript to refer to the row and column location. Often you will use a variable as a subscript, rather than an explicit subscript; for example T(R,C).

When you use a two-dimensional array, you will often use nested FOR-NEXT loops. One loop will take the computer through the rows and the other will take it through the columns. The program on the right creates a two-dimensional array — a multiplication table — with five rows and five columns, using nested FOR-NEXT loops.

You can work with arrays of one, two, or three dimensions on the TI computer. Elements in three-dimensional arrays are referenced with three subscript values: X(22,14,7) or M(I,J,K).

```
>NEW

>100 REM MULTIPLICATION TABLE

>110 CALL CLEAR
>120 CALL CHAR(96,"FF")
>130 CALL CHAR(97,"8080808080
 808080")
>140 CALL CHAR(98,"FF80808080
 808080")
>150 FOR A=1 TO 5
>160 FOR B=1 TO 5
>170 M(A,B)=A*B
>180 NEXT B
>190 NEXT A
>200 FOR A=1 TO 5
>210 FOR B=1 TO 5
>220 PRINT M(A,B);
>230 IF B<>1 THEN 250
>240 PRINT CHR$(97);" ";
>250 NEXT B
>260 PRINT
>270 REM THE FOLLOWING
 STATEMENTS PRINT THE LINES
 DEFINING THE TABLE
>280 IF A<>1 THEN 330
>290 PRINT
>300 CALL HCHAR(23,3,96,3)
>310 CALL HCHAR(23,6,98)
>320 CALL HCHAR(23,7,96,16)
>330 NEXT A
>340 END
>RUN

 -- screen clears
```

1	2	3	4	5
2	4	6	8	10
3	6	9	12	15
4	8	12	16	20
5	10	15	20	25

```
** DONE **
```

DIMension

DIM {array-name (integer1[,integer2][,integer3])},...

The DIMension statement reserves space for both numeric and string arrays. You can explicitly dimension an array only once in your program. If you dimension an array, the DIM statement must appear in the program before any other reference to the array. If you dimension more than one array in a single DIM statement, the array names must be separated by commas. The *array-name* may be any valid variable name.

You may use one-two, or three-dimensional arrays in TI BASIC. The number of values in parentheses following the array name tells the computer how many dimensions the array has.

One-dimensional arrays have only one integer value following their name. Two-dimensional arrays are described with two integer values which define the number of rows and columns. Three-dimensional arrays have three integer values defining their characteristics.

- DIM A(6) — describes a one-dimensional array.
- DIM A(12,3) — describes a two-dimensional array.
- DIM A(5,2,11) — describes a three-dimensional array.

If an array is not dimensioned in a DIM statement, the computer will automatically assign a value of 10 for *integer1* (and a value of 10 for *integer2* and *integer3* if needed) for each array used.

Space is allocated for your array after you enter the RUN command but before the program is actually run. Each element in a string array, however, is a null string until you actually place values in each element. If your computer memory cannot handle an array with the dimensions you specified, you will get a "MEMORY FULL" message and your program will not run.

```
>DIM A(12),B(5)


>NEW

>100 DIM X(15)
>110 FOR I=1 TO 15
>120 READ X(I)
>130 NEXT I
>140 REM PRINT LOOP
>150 FOR I=15 TO 1 STEP -1
>160 PRINT X(I);
>170 NEXT I
>180 DATA 1,2,3,4,5,6,7,8,9,1
 0,11,12,13,14,15
>190 END
>RUN
   15  14  13  12  11  10  9
    8   7   6   5   4   3  2   1
 ** DONE **
```

DIM

Subscripting An Array

Anytime you want to reference an array in your program, you must be specific about which element in the array you want the computer to use. To do this, you point to the element with a *subscript*. Subscripts are enclosed in parentheses immediately following the name of the array. A subscript can be any valid numeric expression which evaluates to a non-negative result. This result will be rounded to the nearest integer, if necessary.

The number of elements reserved for an array determines the maximum value of each subscript for that array. If you are using an array not defined in a DIMension statement, the maximum value of each subscript is 10. The minimum value is zero, unless an OPTION BASE statement sets the minimum subscript value at 1. Thus an array defined as DIM A(6) actually has seven accessible elements in TI BASIC, unless the zero subscript is eliminated by the OPTION BASE 1 statement.

The example on the right assumes that the array begins with element 1 (OPTION BASE 1 on line 120):

- line 130 — This line defines T as a one-dimensional array with 25 elements.

- line 160 — The numeric variable I here subscripts T. Whatever value I contains at this time will be used to point to an element of T. If I=3, the third element of T will be added.

- line 200 — The subscript 14 tells the computer to print the fourteenth element of T.

- line 220 — The computer will evaluate the numeric expression N+2. If N=15 at this time, the seventeenth element of T will be printed.

If you access an array with a subscript greater than the maximum number of elements defined for that array, or if your subscript has a zero value and you used an OPTION BASE 1 statement, a "BAD SUBSCRIPT" message will print and the program will end.

Examples:

```
>NEW

>100 REM DEMO OF DIM AND
 SUBSCRIPTS
>110 S=100
>120 OPTION BASE 1
>130 DIM T(25)
>140 FOR I=1 TO 25
>150 READ T(I)
>160 A=S+T(I)
>170 PRINT A;
>180 NEXT I
>190 PRINT::
>200 PRINT T(14)
>210 INPUT "ENTER A NUMBER BE
 TWEEN 1 AND 23:":N
>220 PRINT T(N+2)
>230 DATA 12,13,43,45,65,76,7
 8,98,56,34,23,21,100,333,222
 ,111,444,666,543,234,89,765,
 90,101,345
>240 END
>RUN
 112   113   143   145   165
 176   178   198   156   134
 123   121   200   443   322
 211   544   766   643   334
 189   865   190   201   445

 333
ENTER A NUMBER BETWEEN 1 AND
 23:14
 111

** DONE **
```

OPTION BASE

OPTION BASE $\left\{ \begin{matrix} 0 \\ 1 \end{matrix} \right\}$

The OPTION BASE statement allows you to set the lower limit of array subscripts at one instead of zero. You can omit the OPTION BASE statement if you want the lower limit of the subscripts to be zero.

If you include an OPTION BASE statement in your program, you must give it a lower line number than any DIMension statement or any reference to an element in any array. You may have only *one* OPTION BASE statement in a program, and it applies to *all* array subscripts in your program. Therefore, you cannot have one array subscript beginning with 0 and another beginning with 1 in the same program.

If you use some integer other than one or zero in the OPTION BASE statement, the computer will stop the program and print "INCORRECT STATEMENT."

```
>NEW

>100 OPTION BASE 1
>110 DIM X(5,5,5)
>120 X(1,0,1)=3
>130 PRINT X(1,0,1)
>140 END
>RUN

  * BAD SUBSCRIPT IN 120

>100 ENTER
>RUN
   3

 ** DONE **
```

Subroutines

Introduction

Subroutines may be thought of as separate self-contained programs within a main program. They usually perform a certain action, such as printing some information, performing a calculation, or reading values into an array. Putting these actions into a subroutine allows you to type that set of statements only once and then perform that set of statements from anywhere in the program with a GOSUB statement.

The GOSUB statement initially behaves like a GOTO statement. It causes the computer to jump to the *line-number* listed. However, subroutine programming gives the computer the capability to "remember" where the branch occurred in the main program and return to that point when it finishes the subroutine. This technique requires that the last statement in the subroutine be a RETURN statement. The program normally has either a STOP statement or some other unconditional branching statement immediately before the subroutines so that the computer doesn't accidentally "fall into" the subroutines. The subroutines should be entered only by a GOSUB instruction and may be entered at any *line-number* within the subroutine.

The example on the right illustrates how the GOSUB and RETURN statements might be arranged in your program. The program begins running at line 100. At line 300 it skips to the first subroutine, performs lines 700 through 780, and returns to line 310. When it reaches line 400, it goes to the second subroutine, performs lines 900 through 980, returns to line 410, and continues running. At line 450 it again goes to subroutine 1, this time entering at line 750 and continuing to the RETURN. Then it goes back to the main program at line 460 and continues running. At line 480 it again jumps to the first subroutine, runs lines 700 through 780, returns to line 490, then stops running at line 600. The STOP statement in line 600 keeps the computer from performing the subroutines unless you specifically direct it there with a GOSUB.

Examples:

```
>NEW

>100 REM MAIN PROGRAM
     .
     .
     .
>300 GOSUB 700
>310 .
     .
     .
>400 GOSUB 900
>410 .
     .
     .
>450 GOSUB 750
>460 .
     .
     .
>480 GOSUB 700
>490 .
     .
     .
>600 STOP
>700 REM SUBROUTINE1
     .
     .
>750 .
     .
     .
>780 RETURN
>900 REM SUBROUTINE2
     .
     .
>980 RETURN
>990 END
```

GOSUB

{ GOSUB   }
{ GO SUB   } *line-number*

The GOSUB statement is used with the RETURN statement to allow you to transfer the program to a subroutine, complete the steps in the subroutine, and return to the next program line following the GOSUB statement. When the computer performs the GOSUB statement, it saves the next line number of the main program so that it can return to that point when it encounters a RETURN statement in the subroutine.

(The space between GO and SUB is optional.)

Examples:

```
>NEW

>100 REM BUILD AN ARRAY,
 MULTIPLY EACH ELEMENT BY 3,
 PRINT BOTH ARRAYS
>110 FOR X=1 TO 4
>120 FOR Y=1 TO 7
>130 I(X,Y)=INT(30*RND)+1
>140 NEXT Y
>150 NEXT X
>160 PRINT "FIRST ARRAY":
>170 GOSUB 260
>180 FOR X=1 TO 4
>190 FOR Y=1 TO 7
>200 I(X,Y)=3*I(X,Y)
>210 NEXT Y
>220 NEXT X
>230 PRINT "3 TIMES VALUES IN
 FIRST ARRAY"::
>240 GOSUB 260
>250 STOP
>260 REM SUBROUTINE TO PRINT
 ARRAY
>270 FOR X=1 TO 4
>280 FOR Y=1 TO 7
>290 PRINT I(X,Y);
>300 NEXT Y
>310 PRINT
>320 NEXT X
>330 PRINT
>340 RETURN
>RUN
 FIRST ARRAY

 16   12   17   12    8   17    8
 18   22    1   29   16   14   11
  5   25   22    4   24   11   24
 26   21   18    2   12   20   15

 3 TIMES VALUES IN FIRST ARRA
 Y

 48   36   51   36   24   51   24
 54   66    3   87   48   42   33
 15   75   66   12   72   33   72
 78   63   54    6   36   60   45

 ** DONE **
```

GOSUB

Within a subroutine, you may want the computer to jump to another subroutine, complete it, come back to the first subroutine, complete its steps, then return to the main program at the point where the original branch occurred. You can do this easily with the proper pairing of GOSUB and RETURN statements. However, be sure you exercise care in designing subroutines so that the computer will not "lose its place."

In the example on the right, the main program jumps to subroutine 1 when it reaches line 500. In subroutine 1, when the program reaches line 730, it goes to subroutine 2. When the RETURN in subroutine 2 is encountered (line 850), the computer returns to subroutine 1 at line 740, finishes the subroutine, returns to the main program and completes it through line 600.

If the GOSUB statement transfers the program to a *line-number* not in the program, the program will end and the message "BAD LINE NUMBER" will print. If the GOSUB transfers the program to its own *line-number,* the program will stop and the message "MEMORY FULL" will print.

Examples:

```
>NEW

>100 REM NESTED SUBROUTINES
>110 REM MAIN PROGRAM
     .
     .
     .
>500 GOSUB 700
>510 .
     .
     .
>600 STOP
>700 REM SUBROUTINE1
     .
     .
     .
>730 GOSUB 800
>740 .
     .
     .
>790 RETURN
>800 REM SUBROUTINE2
     .
     .
     .
>850 RETURN
```

```
>NEW

>100 X=12
>110 Y=23
>120 GOSUB 120
>130 PRINT Z
>140 STOP
>150 REM SUBROUTINE
>160 Z=X+Y*120/5
>170 RETURN
>RUN

* MEMORY FULL IN 120

>120 GOSUB 150
>RUN
  564

** DONE **
```

RETURN

RETURN

The RETURN statement is used with the GOSUB statement
to provide a branch and return structure for TI BASIC.
Whenever the computer encounters a RETURN statement, it takes
the program back to the program line immediately following the
GOSUB statement that transferred the computer to that particular
subroutine in the first place. You can easily develop programs with
subroutines which jump to other subroutines and back again, if you
are careful that each GOSUB leads the computer to a RETURN
statement.

If, when running a program, the computer encounters a RETURN
statement before performing a GOSUB instruction, the program
will terminate with the message "CAN'T DO THAT."

Examples:

```
>NEW

>100 FOR I=1 TO 3
>110 GOSUB 150
>120 PRINT "I=";I
>130 NEXT I
>140 STOP
>150 REM SUBROUTINE
>160 FOR X=1 TO 2
>170 PRINT "X=";X
>180 NEXT X
>190 RETURN
>RUN
 X= 1
 X= 2
 I= 1
 X= 1
 X= 2
 I= 2
 X= 1
 X= 2
 I= 3

** DONE **
```

ON-GOSUB

ON *numeric-expression* $\begin{Bmatrix} \text{GOSUB} \\ \text{GO SUB} \end{Bmatrix}$ *line-number* [,*line-number*] . . .

The ON-GOSUB statement is used with the RETURN statement to tell the computer to perform one of several subroutines, depending on the value of a *numeric-expression*, and then go back to the main program sequence.

The computer first evaluates the *numeric-expression* and converts the result to an integer, rounding if necessary. This integer tells the program which subroutine *line-number* in the ON-GOSUB statement to perform next. If the value of the *numeric-expression* is 1, the computer will proceed to the first *line-number* listed in the ON-GOSUB statement. If the value is 2, the computer will branch to the second *line-number* given, and so on.

Additionally the computer will save the next line number following the ON-GOSUB statement and return to this point after performing the subroutine. The subroutine must contain a RETURN statement to signal the computer to go back to the saved line number and continue the program from that statement. Otherwise, the program will continue until it reaches the end, as if a GOTO was performed instead of a GOSUB.

If the rounded value of the *numeric-expression* is less than 1 or greater than the number of line numbers in the ON-GOSUB statement, the program will terminate with the message "BAD VALUE IN xx."

If the *line-number* listed is not a valid program line, the message "BAD LINE NUMBER" will print when you perform the statement.

Examples:

```
>NEW

>100 INPUT "CODE=?":CODE
>110 IF CODE=9 THEN 290
>120 INPUT "HOURS=?":HOURS
>130 ON CODE GOSUB 170,200,23
0,260
>140 PAY=RATE*HOURS+BASEPAY
>150 PRINT "PAY IS $";PAY
>160 GOTO 100
>170 RATE=3.10
>180 BASEPAY=5
>190 RETURN
>200 RATE=4.25
>210 BASEPAY=25
>220 RETURN
>230 RATE=10
>240 BASEPAY=50
>250 RETURN
>260 RATE=25
>270 BASEPAY=100
>280 RETURN
>290 END
>RUN
 CODE=?4
 HOURS=?40
 PAY IS $ 1100
 CODE=?2
 HOURS=?37
 PAY IS $ 182.25
 CODE=?3
 HOURS=?35.75
 PAY IS $ 407.5
 CODE=?1
 HOURS=?40
 PAY IS $ 129
 CODE=?9

 ** DONE **


>RUN
 CODE=?5
 HOURS=?40

 * BAD VALUE IN 130


>130 ON CODE GOSUB 170,200,23
0,600
>RUN
 CODE=?4
 HOURS=?40

 * BAD LINE NUMBER IN 130
```

File Processing

Introduction

Your TI computer has the capability to store both programs and data on accessory devices. You can later load and use these files with your computer as often as you wish, and delete them when you no longer need them.

The file-processing capability of your computer offers you a powerful programming tool. You can eliminate retyping your favorite programs, save important information, and create procedures to update data important to you. TI BASIC provides an extensive range of file-processing features, including sequential and random file organization and processing, fixed and variable length records, and display and internal formats for data. This section describes the TI BASIC statements which use these features — OPEN, CLOSE, INPUT, PRINT, and RESTORE. As new accessory devices become available, the file features they use will be described in the accompanying manuals.

Note: Device names in TI BASIC are generally required to be upper-case letters. For example,

> DSK1.*filename*
> CS1
> RS232

Audio Cassette Tape Recorders

Your TI computer can process files from either one or two standard audio cassette tape recorders (see the "Cassette Interface Cable" section of this book for instructions on attaching the recorders). These recorders are designated as CS1 and CS2. To save and/or load programs you need only one recorder. To read data from a file, process it in your program, and at the same time create a new data file, you will need two recorders — one to read the stored data and one to write the processed data.

Specific requirements for using file processing features with cassette recorders are given at the end of each statement description.

TI Disk Memory System

A disk system, consisting of the TI Disk Drive Controller and one to three Disk Memory Drives, is also available for rapid, accurate data storage and retrieval. The system uses 5¼-inch, single-sided, single-density, soft-sectored diskettes.

A Disk Manager Command Module is enclosed with the Disk Drive Controller, allowing you to perform easily certain disk operations, such as cataloging, renaming files, and protecting files. For more details, see the owner's manual that accompanies the controller.

OPEN

OPEN #*file-number:file-name*[,*file-organization*][,*file-type*][,*open-mode*][,*record-type*][,*file-life*]

The OPEN statement prepares a BASIC program to use data files stored on accessory devices. The OPEN statement does this by providing the necessary link between a *file-number* used in your program and the particular accessory device on which the file is located.

The OPEN statement describes a file's characteristics to the computer so that your program can process it or create it. With some accessory devices the computer will check that the file or device characteristics match the information specified in the OPEN statement for that file. If they don't match or the computer cannot find or create the file, the file will not be opened and an I/O error message will be printed.

The *file-number* and *file-name* must be included in the OPEN statement. The other information can be included in any order or can be omitted. If you leave out any specification, the computer will assume certain standard characteristics for the file, called "defaults," as described later in this section.

■ *file-number* — All TI BASIC statements which refer to files do so by means of a *file-number* between 0 and 255 inclusive. The *file-number* is assigned to a particular file by the OPEN statement. Since *file-number* 0 refers to the keyboard and screen of your computer and is always accessible, you cannot open or close *file-number* 0 in your program statements. You may assign the other numbers as you wish, as long as each open file in your program has a different number.

The *file-number* is entered as the number sign (#) followed by a numeric expression. When the computer evaluates this expression and rounds the answer to the nearest integer, the number must be 1 to 255 inclusive and cannot be the same *file-number* as any other file you are using concurrently in the program.

■ *file-name* — A *file-name* refers to a device or to a file located on a device, depending on the capability of the accessory. Each accessory has a predefined name which the computer recognizes. For example, the valid *file-names* for the two audio cassette recorders are "CS1" and "CS2." By including this *file-name* in the OPEN statement, you are telling the computer to access a particular file or device whenever the program references the associated *file-number*. The *file-name* can be any string expression which evaluates to a valid *file-name*. If you use a string constant, you must enclose it in quotes.

Examples:

```
>100 OPEN #2:"CS1",SEQUENTIAL
,INTERNAL,INPUT,FIXED 128,PE
RMANENT
```

```
>100 OPEN #25:"CS1",SEQUENTIA
L,INTERNAL,INPUT,FIXED,PERMA
NENT
>110 X=100
>120 OPEN #X+5:"CS2",SEQUENTI
AL,INTERNAL,OUTPUT,FIXED,PER
MANENT
```

```
>130 N=2
>140 OPEN #122:"CS"&STR$(N),S
EQUENTIAL,INTERNAL,OUTPUT,FI
XED,PERMANENT
```

OPEN

Information about the *file-names* associated with the TI Disk Memory System, the RS232 Interface, and other accessories is included in the manuals which accompany them.

- *file-organization* — Files used in TI BASIC can be organized either sequentially or randomly. Records on a sequential file are read or written one after the other in sequence from beginning to end. Random-access files (called RELATIVE in TI BASIC) can be read or written in any record order. They may also be processed sequentially.

  To indicate which logical structure a file has, enter either SEQUENTIAL or RELATIVE in the OPEN statement. You may optionally specify the initial number of records on a file by following the word SEQUENTIAL or RELATIVE with a numeric expression.

  If you omit the *file-organization* specification, the computer will assume SEQUENTIAL organization.

- *file-type* — This specification designates the format of the data stored on the file: DISPLAY or INTERNAL.

  The DISPLAY-type format refers to printable (ASCII) characters. The DISPLAY format is normally used when the output will be read by people, rather than by the computer. Each DISPLAY-type record usually corresponds to one print line.

  INTERNAL-type data is recorded in internal machine format which has not been translated into printable characters. Data in this form can be read easily by the computer but not by people. (See "INPUT" for a full explanation of how data is stored internally.)

  You will find that the INTERNAL format is more efficient for recording data on a storage device such as a cassette tape. It requires less space and is easier to format with a PRINT statement (see "PRINT" for directions on formatting PRINT statements for INTERNAL-type records and for DISPLAY-type records). Because the computer uses INTERNAL-type data internally, a program runs in less time when your data files are in INTERNAL format. The computer won't have to convert DISPLAY characters into INTERNAL format and back again.

  If this specification is omitted, the computer assumes DISPLAY format.

Examples:

```
>100 OPEN #4:"CS2",OUTPUT,INT
ERNAL,SEQUENTIAL,FIXED
```

```
>120 OPEN #12:NAME$,RELATIVE
50,INPUT,FIXED,INTERNAL
```

```
>100 OPEN #10:"CS1",OUTPUT,FI
XED
```

```
(computer assumes SEQUENTIAL
DISPLAY,PERMANENT)
```

■ *open-mode* – This entry instructs the computer to process the file in the INPUT, OUTPUT, UPDATE or APPEND mode. If you omit this clause, the computer will assume the UPDATE mode.

- INPUT files may be read only.

- OUTPUT files may be written only. The new file created will have all the characteristics given by the OPEN statement specifications and any standard defaults.

- UPDATE files may be both read and written. The usual processing is to read a record, change it in some way, and then write the altered record back out on the file.

- APPEND mode allows data to be added at the end of the existing file. The records already on the file cannot be accessed in this mode.

■ *record-type* – This entry specifies whether the records on the file are all the same length (FIXED) or vary in length (VARIABLE). The keyword FIXED or VARIABLE may be followed by a numeric expression specifying the maximum length of a record. Each accessory device has its own maximum record length, so be sure to check the manuals which accompany them. If you omit the record-length specification, the computer will assume a record length depending upon the device used.

If you define a file as RELATIVE, you must use FIXED-length records. If this entry is omitted for RELATIVE files, FIXED-length records are assumed, with the length dependent on the device.

SEQUENTIAL files may have FIXED or VARIABLE length records. If this entry is omitted for SEQUENTIAL files, VARIABLE-length records are assumed.

If records are FIXED, the computer will pad each record on the right to ensure that it is the specified length. If the data is recorded in DISPLAY format, the computer will pad the record with spaces. If the INTERNAL format is used, the FIXED-length record will be padded with binary zeroes.

■ *file-life* – Files you create with your TI Computer are considered PERMANENT, not temporary. You may omit this entry entirely, since the computer will assume a PERMANENT file-life.

Examples:

```
>100 OPEN #53:NAME$,FIXED,INT
ERNAL,RELATIVE
```

(computer assumes UPDATE)

```
>100 OPEN #11:NAME$,INPUT,INT
ERNAL,SEQUENTIAL,VARIABLE 10
0

>100 OPEN #75:"CS1",OUTPUT,FI
XED
```

(computer assumes SEQUENTIAL, DISPLAY,FIXED length of 64 positions)

OPEN

Cassette Recorder Information

- *file-number** — any number between 1 and 255 inclusive
- *file-name** — "CS1" or "CS2"
- *file-organization* — SEQUENTIAL
- *file-type* — INTERNAL (preferred) or DISPLAY
- *open-mode** — INPUT or OUTPUT
- *record-type** — FIXED

*This specification is required.

For cassette tape records, you may specify any length up to 192 positions. However, the cassette tape device uses records with 64, 128, or 192 positions and will pad the record you specify to the appropriate length. Thus, if you specify an 83-position cassette record, the computer will actually write a 128-position record. If the record length is not specified, a 64-position record length is assumed.

For cassette devices, the computer does not compare the file specifications in the OPEN statement to the characteristics of an existing file.

Whenever the computer performs the OPEN statement for a cassette tape device, you will receive instructions on your screen for activating the recorder, as shown on the right.

Note: Only "CS1" can be specified for an INPUT file. Both "CS1" and "CS2" can be used for OUTPUT files.

Examples:

```
>NEW

>100 OPEN #2:"CS1",INTERNAL,I
NPUT,FIXED
.
. program lines
.
>290 CLOSE #2
>300 END
>RUN

* REWIND CASSETTE TAPE   CS1
  THEN PRESS ENTER

* PRESS CASSETTE PLAY    CS1
  THEN PRESS ENTER
.
. rest of program run
.
* PRESS CASSETTE STOP    CS1
  THEN PRESS ENTER

** DONE **
```

CLOSE

CLOSE #*file-number*[:DELETE]

The CLOSE statement "closes" or discontinues the association
between a file and a program. After the CLOSE statement is
performed, the "closed" file is not available to your program unless
you OPEN it again. Also, the computer will no longer associate the
closed file with the *file-number* you specified in the program. You
can then assign that particular *file-number* to any file you wish.

If you use the DELETE option in the CLOSE statement, the
action performed depends on the device used. As additional
accessory devices become available, their accompanying manuals
will describe the DELETE option.

If you attempt to CLOSE a file that you have not opened previously
in your program, the computer will terminate your program with
the "FILE ERROR" message.

In order to safeguard your files, the computer will automatically
close any open files should an error occur which terminates your
program. If a break occurs in your program, either by a BREAK
command or your pressing **CLEAR**, open files are automatically
closed *only* if one of the following occurs:

- you edit the program
- you terminate BASIC with the BYE command
- you RUN the program again
- you enter a NEW command

If you use **QUIT** to leave your program, the computer will *NOT*
close any open files and you could lose the data on these files. If
you need to exit from your file-processing program before its
normal end, follow these directions so that you won't lose any data:

- Press **CLEAR** until the computer reacts with
  "BREAKPOINT AT xx." This may take
  several seconds.
- Enter BYE when the cursor reappears on the screen.

Examples:

```
>NEW

>100 OPEN #6:"CS1",SEQUENTIAL
 ,INTERNAL,INPUT,FIXED
>110 OPEN #25:"CS2",SEQUENTIA
 L,INTERNAL,OUTPUT,FIXED

 . program lines

>200 CLOSE #6:DELETE
>210 CLOSE #25
>220 END
```

CLOSE

Cassette Recorder Information

Whenever the computer performs the CLOSE statement for a cassette tape device, you will receive instructions on your screen for operating the recorder, as shown on the right.

If you use the DELETE option with cassette recorders, no action beyond the closing of the file takes place.

Examples:

```
>NEW

>100 OPEN #24:"CS1",INTERNAL,
 INPUT,FIXED
>110 OPEN #19:"CS2",INTERNAL,
 OUTPUT,FIXED
 .
 . program lines
 .
>200 CLOSE #24
>210 CLOSE #19
>220 END
>RUN

 * REWIND CASSETTE TAPE    CS1
   THEN PRESS ENTER

 * PRESS CASSETTE PLAY     CS1
   THEN PRESS ENTER

 * REWIND CASSETTE TAPE    CS2
   THEN PRESS ENTER

 * PRESS CASSETTE RECORD   CS2
   THEN PRESS ENTER
   .
   . program runs
   .

 * PRESS CASSETTE STOP     CS1
   THEN PRESS ENTER

 * PRESS CASSETTE STOP     CS2
   THEN PRESS ENTER

 ** DONE **
```

INPUT

INPUT #*file-number*,REC *numeric-expression*:*variable-list*

(See also the "Input-Output Statements" section.)

This form of the INPUT statement allows you to read data from an accessory device. The INPUT statement can be used only with files opened in INPUT or UPDATE mode. The *file-number* in the INPUT statement must be the *file-number* of a currently open file. *File-number* 0, the keyboard, may always be used. If you choose to use *file-number* 0, the INPUT statement is performed as described in "Input-Output Statements," except that you cannot specify an input-prompt.

The *variable-list* contains those variables which are assigned values when the INPUT statement is performed. Variable names in the *variable-list* are separated by commas and may be numeric and/or string variables.

Filling the variable-list

When the computer reads records from a file, it stores each complete record internally in a temporary storage area called an input/output (I/O) buffer. A separate buffer is provided for each open *file-number*. Values are assigned to variables in the *variable-list* from left to right, using the data in this buffer. Whenever a *variable-list* has been filled with corresponding values, any data items left in the buffer are discarded unless the INPUT statement ends with a trailing comma. Using a trailing comma creates a "pending" input condition (see "Using Pending Inputs").

If the *variable-list* in the INPUT statement is longer than the number of data items in the current record being processed, the computer will get the next record from the file and use its data items to complete the *variable-list*, as shown on the right.

When performing the INPUT statement, the computer will take different actions depending on whether the data stored is in DISPLAY or INTERNAL format.

```
>NEW

>100 OPEN #13:"CS1",SEQUENTIA
L,DISPLAY,INPUT,FIXED
>110 INPUT #13:A,B,C$,D$,X,Y,
Z$
>120 IF A=99 THEN 150
>130 PRINT A;B:C$:D$:X;Y:Z$
>140 GOTO 110
>150 CLOSE #13
>160 END
>RUN

  --data stored on tape will be
    printed on the screen

  ** DONE **
```

```
>NEW

>100 OPEN #13:"CS1",SEQUENTIA
L,DISPLAY,INPUT,FIXED 64
>110 INPUT #13:A,B,C,D
 .
 . program lines
 .
>290 CLOSE #13
>300 END
>RUN

  --1st INPUT RECORD=22,77,56,
                      92

  --Results:
     A=22  B=77  C=56  D=92
```

```
>NEW

>100 OPEN #13:"CS1",SEQUENTIA
L,DISPLAY,INPUT,FIXED 64
>110 INPUT #13:A,B,C,D,E,F,G
 .
 . program lines
 .
>400 END

  --1ST INPUT RECORD=22,33.5
  --2ND INPUT RECORD=405,92
  --3RD INPUT RECORD=-22,11023
  --4TH INPUT RECORD=99,100

  --Results:

  A=22  B=33.5  C=405  D=92

  E=-22 F=11023 G=99
```

INPUT

DISPLAY-type Data

DISPLAY-type data has the same form as data entered from the keyboard. The computer knows the length of each data item in a DISPLAY-type record by the comma separators placed between items.

Each item in a DISPLAY-type record is checked to ensure that numeric values are placed in numeric variables as shown on the right in record 1. If the data-type doesn't match the variable-type, as in Record 2 on the right (JG is not a numeric value), an INPUT ERROR will occur and the program will terminate.

INTERNAL-type Data

INTERNAL-type data has the following form:

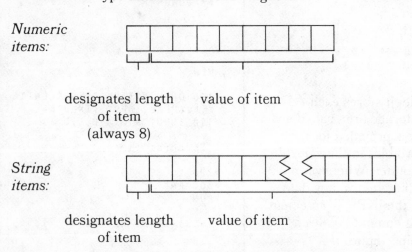

Numeric items:

designates length of item (always 8)   value of item

String items:

designates length of item   value of item

The computer knows the length of each INTERNAL-type item by interpreting the one-position length indicator at the beginning of each item.

Limited validation of INTERNAL-type data-items is performed. All numeric items must be 9 positions long (8 digits plus one position which specifies the length) and must be valid representations of floating-point numbers. Otherwise, an INPUT ERROR will occur, and the program will terminate.

For FIXED-length INTERNAL records, reading beyond the actual data recorded in each record will cause padding characters (binary zeros) to be read. If you attempt to assign these characters to a numeric variable, an INPUT ERROR occurs. If strings are being read, a null string is assigned to the string variable.

```
>NEW

>100 OPEN #13:"CS1",SEQUENTIA
 L,DISPLAY,INPUT,FIXED 64
>110 INPUT #13:A,B,STATE$,D$,
 X,Y

  --INPUT RECORD 1=22,97.6,
    TEXAS,"AUTO LICENSE ",
    22000,-.07

  --INPUT RECORD 2=JG,22,TEXAS
    PROPERTY TAX,42,15
```

INPUT

Using INPUT with RELATIVE Files

(See "OPEN" for a description of RELATIVE file-organization.)

You may read RELATIVE files either sequentially or randomly. The computer sets up an internal counter to point to which record should be processed next. The first record in a file is record 0. Thus, the counter begins at zero and is incremented by +1 after each access to the file, either to read or to write a record. In the example on the right, the statements direct the computer to read the file sequentially.

The internal counter can be changed by using the REC clause. The *numeric-expression* following the keyword REC will be evaluated to designate a specific record number on the file. When the computer performs an INPUT statement with a REC clause, it reads the specified record from the designated file and places it in the I/O buffer. The REC clause can appear only in statements referencing RELATIVE files. The example on the right illustrates accessing a RELATIVE file randomly, using the REC clause.

Be sure to use the REC clause if you read and write records on the same file within a program. Since the same internal counter is incremented when records are either read or written for the same file, you may skip some records and write over others if REC is not used, as shown in the example on the right.

If the internal counter points to a record beyond the limits of the file when the computer tries to access the file, the program will terminate with an INPUT ERROR.

Examples:

```
>NEW

>100 OPEN #4:NAME$,RELATIVE,I
NTERNAL,INPUT,FIXED 64
>110 INPUT #4:A,B,C$,D$,X
 .
 . program lines
 .
>200 CLOSE #4
>210 END


>NEW

>100 OPEN #6:NAME$,RELATIVE,I
NTERNAL,UPDATE,FIXED 72
>110 INPUT K
>120 INPUT #6,REC K:A,B,C$,D$
 .
 . program lines
 .
>170 PRINT #6,REC K:A,B,C$,D$
 .
 . program lines
 .
>300 CLOSE #6
>310 END


>NEW

>100 OPEN #3:NAME$,RELATIVE,I
NTERNAL,UPDATE,FIXED
>110 FOR I=1 TO 10
>120 INPUT #3:A$,B$,C$,X,Y
 .
 . program lines
 .
>230 PRINT #3:A$,B$,C$,X,Y
>240 NEXT I
>250 CLOSE #3
>260 END
>RUN

 --LINE 120-Reads records
          0,2,4,6,8...

 --LINE 130-Writes records
          1,3,5,7,9...
```

INPUT

Using Pending Inputs

A pending input condition is established when an INPUT statement with a trailing comma is performed. When the next INPUT statement using that file is encountered, one of the following actions will occur:

- If the next INPUT statement has no REC clause — the computer uses the data in the I/O buffer beginning where the previous INPUT statement stopped.
- If the next INPUT statement includes a REC clause — the computer terminates the pending input condition and reads the specified record into the file's I/O buffer.

If a pending input condition exists and a PRINT statement for the same file is performed, the pending input condition is terminated and the PRINT statement is performed as usual.

If you use a pending input with *file-number* 0, the error message "INCORRECT STATEMENT" is printed and the program stops running.

End-of-file

In sequential processing, to prevent an error when the computer has no more data to read, you will need to notify the computer that the end of the file has been reached. To make this easier for you, TI BASIC includes an End-of-File function called EOF. Be sure to include the EOF statement immediately before the INPUT statement which reads a sequential file. In this way you can easily cause the computer to stop reading the input file when no more data is available. The usual procedure is to skip to a closing routine when EOF is reached.

```
>NEW

>100 INPUT #0:A,B,
>110 PRINT A;B
>120 GOTO 100
>RUN
 ?
 * INCORRECT STATEMENT
   IN 100


>NEW

>100 OPEN #5:NAME$,SEQUENTIAL
 ,INTERNAL,INPUT,FIXED
>110 IF EOF(5) THEN 150
>120 INPUT #5:A,B
>130 PRINT A;B
>140 GOTO 110
>150 CLOSE #5
>160 END
```

INPUT

The EOF function cannot be used with RELATIVE files or with some accessory devices. In these cases, you will need to create your own method for determining that the end-of-file has been reached.

One common end-of-file technique is to create a last record on the file that serves as an end-of-file indicator. It is called a "dummy" record because the data it contains is used only to mark the end of the file. For example, it could be filled with "9's." Whenever the computer inputs a record, you can check the data. If it is equal to "9's," then the computer has reached end-of-file and can skip to the closing routine.

The first example on the right creates a dummy record. In the next example, the computer checks for the dummy record as its end-of-file technique.

Cassette Recorder Information

- RELATIVE file-organization cannot be used with cassette devices.
- The EOF (End-of-File) function cannot be used with files on cassette recorders.
- You may specify a record length up to 192 positions (see "OPEN").
- Only cassette unit 1 (CS1) can be used for inputting data.

Examples:

```
>NEW

>100 OPEN #2:"CS1",SEQUENTIAL
,FIXED,OUTPUT,INTERNAL
>110 READ A,B,C
>120 IF A=99 THEN 180
>130 E=A+B+C
>140 PRINT A;B;C;E
>150 PRINT #2:A,B,C,E
>160 GOTO 110
>170 DATA 5,10,15,10,20,30,10
0,200,300,99,99,99
>180 PRINT #2:99,99,99,99
>190 CLOSE #2
>200 END
>RUN


 * REWIND CASSETTE TAPE    CS1
   THEN PRESS ENTER

 * PRESS CASSETTE RECORD   CS1
   THEN PRESS ENTER
   5    10   15   30
   10   20   30   60
   100  200  300  600

 * PRESS CASSETTE STOP     CS1
   THEN PRESS ENTER

 ** DONE **


>NEW

>100 OPEN #1:"CS1",INTERNAL,I
NPUT,FIXED
>110 INPUT #1:A,B,C,E
>120 IF A=99 THEN 160
>130 F=A*E
>140 PRINT A;B;C;E;F
>150 GOTO 110
>160 CLOSE #1
>170 END
>RUN


 * REWIND CASSETTE TAPE    CS1
   THEN PRESS ENTER

 * PRESS CASSETTE PLAY     CS1
   THEN PRESS ENTER
   5    10   15   30   150
   10   20   30   60   600
   100  200  300  600  6000

 * PRESS CASSETTE STOP     CS1
   THEN PRESS ENTER

 ** DONE **
```

EOF—End-of-File Function

EOF (*numeric-expression*)

The end-of-file function determines if an end-of-file has been reached on a file stored on an accessory device. The argument specifies an open file-number (see "OPEN"). The argument is the value obtained when the *numeric-expression* is evaluated. The normal rules for the evaluation of numeric expressions are used here.

The value the function provides depends on the position of the file. The values supplied are:

Value	Position
0	Not end-of-file
+1	Logical end-of-file
−1	Physical end-of-file

A file is positioned at a logical end-of-file when all records on the file have been processed. A file is positioned at a physical end-of-file when no more space is available for the file.

This function and the example on the right cannot be used with cassette tape recorders. Its use with any other accessory devices will be more fully explained in their accompanying manuals.

Examples:

```
>NEW

>100 OPEN #2:NAME$,SEQUENTIAL
,INTERNAL,INPUT,FIXED
>110 IF EOF(2) THEN 160
>120 REM IF EOF GIVES ZERO
>130 INPUT #2:A,B,C
>140 PRINT A;B;C
>150 GOTO 110
>160 CLOSE #2
>170 END
```

PRINT

PRINT #*file-number*[,REC *numeric-expression*][:*print-list*]

(For a description of the PRINT format for printing on the computer screen, see the "Input-Output Statements" section.)

This form of the PRINT statement allows you to write data onto an accessory device. The PRINT statement can be used to write only on files opened in OUTPUT, UPDATE, or APPEND mode. The *file-number* must be the *file-number* of a currently open file.

When the computer performs a PRINT statement, it stores the data in a temporary storage area called an input/output (I/O) buffer. A separate buffer is provided for each open *file-number*. If the PRINT statement does not end with a print-separator (comma, semicolon, or colon), the record is immediately written onto the file from the I/O buffer. If the PRINT statement ends with a print-separator, the data is held in the buffer and a "pending" print condition occurs (see "Using Pending Prints" in this section.)

The information you need for creating a *print-list* to record data on accessory file storage devices is discussed here. The *print-list* needed to display print lines (on a printer, etc.) is the same as the *print-list* described in "Input-Output Statements." You may use either DISPLAY or INTERNAL format for data stored on accessory devices. However, since these files are read only by the computer, by far the easiest-to-use and most efficient data-type is INTERNAL.

Using PRINT with INTERNAL-type Data

The *print-list* consists of numeric and string expressions separated by commas, colons, or semicolons. All print-separators in a *print-list* have the same effect for INTERNAL-type data — they only separate the items from each other and do not indicate spacing character positions in a record.

Examples:

```
>NEW

>100 OPEN #5:"CS1",SEQUENTIAL
,INTERNAL,OUTPUT,FIXED
 .
 . program lines
 .
>170 PRINT #5:A,B,C$,D$
 .
 . program lines
 .
>200 CLOSE #5
>210 END
```

```
>NEW

>100 OPEN #6:"CS2",SEQUENTIAL
,DISPLAY,OUTPUT,FIXED
 .
 . program lines
 .
>170 PRINT #6:A;",";B;",";C$;
",";D$
 .
 . program lines
 .
>200 CLOSE #6
>210 END
```

PRINT

When items in the *print-list* are written on the accessory storage device in INTERNAL format, they have the following characteristics:

Numeric items:

designates length value of item
of item
(always 8)

String items:

designates length value of item
of item

In the example on the right, the total length of the data recorded in INTERNAL format is 71 positions. Each numeric variable uses 9 positions. A$ is 18 characters long (line 110) plus 1 position to record the length of the string. B$ is 15 characters (line 120) plus 1. If the values of A$ and B$ change during the program, their lengths will vary according to whatever value is present when the record is written onto the files. In designing your record, therefore, become familiar with the data each variable might contain and plan your record to allow for the largest length possible.

Whenever you specify FIXED-length records, the computer will pad each INTERNAL-type record with binary zeros, if necessary, to bring each record to the specified length.

The computer will not allow a record to be longer than the specified or default length for the device you are using. If including all data in a *print-list* would cause this condition to occur for an INTERNAL-type record, the program will terminate with the message "FILE ERROR IN xx."

Examples:

```
>NEW

>100 OPEN #5:"CS1",SEQUENTIAL
,INTERNAL,OUTPUT,FIXED 128
>110 A$="TEXAS INSTRUMENTS "
>120 B$="COMPUTER "
>130 READ X,Y,Z
>140 IF X=99 THEN 190
>150 A=X*Y*Z
>160 PRINT #5:A$,X,Y,Z,B$,A
>170 GOTO 130
>180 DATA 5,6,7,1,2,3,10,20,3
0,20,40,60,1.5,2.3,7.6,99,99
,99
>190 CLOSE #5
>200 END
>RUN


* REWIND CASSETTE TAPE      CS1
  THEN PRESS ENTER

* PRESS CASSETTE RECORD     CS1
  THEN PRESS ENTER

--data written on tape

* PRESS CASSETTE STOP       CS1
  THEN PRESS ENTER

** DONE **
```

PRINT

Using PRINT with DISPLAY-type Data on File Storage Devices

Although it is best to use INTERNAL format for data recorded on file storage devices which will be read by the computer, you may occasionally need to use DISPLAY-type records. Included here are several important considerations you must observe when using DISPLAY format.

- Records are created according to the specifications found in the PRINT statement of the "Input-Output Statements" section.

- If including a data-item from the *print-list* would cause the record to be longer than the specified or default length for the device you are using, the item is not split but becomes the first item in the next record. If any single item is longer than the record length, the item will be split into as many records as required to store it. The program continues running normally and no warning is given.

- In order to later read DISPLAY-type files created with the PRINT statement, the data must look like it does when you enter it from the keyboard. Therefore, you must explicitly include the comma separators and quote marks needed by the INPUT statement when you write the record on the file. These punctuation marks are not automatically inserted when the PRINT statement is performed. They must be included as items in the *print-list*, as shown in line 170 on the right.

- Numeric items *do not* have a fixed length as they do in INTERNAL format. In DISPLAY-type files, the length of a numeric item is the same as it would be if it were displayed on the screen using the PRINT or DISPLAY statement (i.e., includes sign, decimal point, exponent, trailing space, etc.). For example, the number of positions required to print 1.35E-10 is ten.

Examples:

```
>NEW

>100 OPEN #10:"CS1",SEQUENTIA
L,DISPLAY,OUTPUT,FIXED 128
.
. program lines
.
>170 PRINT #10:"""";A$;""","";
X;",";Y;",";Z;",""";B$;""","
;A
.
. program lines
.
>300 CLOSE #10
>310 END
```

PRINT

Using PRINT with RELATIVE Files

(See "OPEN" for a description of RELATIVE file-organization.)

RELATIVE file records can be processed randomly or in sequence. The computer sets up an internal counter to point to which record should be processed next. The first record in a file is record 0. Thus, the counter begins at zero and is incremented by +1 after each file access, either to read or to write a record. In the example on the right, the PRINT statement directs the computer to write the file sequentially. It can later be processed either randomly or in sequence.

The internal counter can be changed by using the REC clause. The keyword REC must be followed by a *numeric-expression* whose value specifies in which position the record in the file is to be written. When the computer performs a PRINT statement with a REC clause, it begins building an output record in the I/O buffer. When this record is written onto the file, it will be placed at the location specified by the REC clause. You may use the REC clause only with RELATIVE files. The example on the right illustrates writing records randomly, using the REC clause.

Be sure to use the REC clause if you read and write records on the same file within a program. Since the same internal counter is incremented when records are either read or written for the same file, you could skip some records and write over others if REC is not used, as shown in the example on the right.

Examples:

```
>NEW

>100 OPEN #3:NAME$,RELATIVE,I
NTERNAL,OUTPUT,FIXED 128
 .
 . program lines
 .
>150 PRINT #3:A$,B$,C$,X,Y,Z
 .
 . program lines
 .
>200 CLOSE #3
>210 END
```

```
>NEW

>100 OPEN #3:NAME$,RELATIVE,I
NTERNAL,UPDATE,FIXED 128
>110 INPUT K
>120 PRINT #3,REC K:A$,B$,C$,
X,Y,Z
 .
 . program lines
 .
>300 CLOSE #3
>310 END
```

```
>NEW

>100 OPEN #3:NAME$,RELATIVE,I
NTERNAL,UPDATE,FIXED
>110 FOR I=1 TO 10
>120 INPUT #3:A$,B$,C$,X,Y
>130 PRINT #3:A$,B$,C$,X,Y
>140 NEXT I
>150 CLOSE #3
>160 END

  LINE 120-reads records 0,2,4,
                         6,8...

  LINE 130-writes records 1,3,
                          5,7,
                          9...
```

PRINT

Using Pending Prints

A record is always written onto a file whenever the computer performs a PRINT statement which has no trailing separator. A pending print condition is established when a PRINT statement with a trailing print-separator is performed. When the next PRINT statement using the file is encountered, one of the following actions occurs:

- If the next PRINT statement has no REC clause — the computer places the data in the I/O buffer immediately following the data already there.
- If the next PRINT statement has a REC clause — the computer writes the pending print record onto the file at the position indicated by the internal counter and performs the new PRINT-REC statement as usual.

If a pending print condition exists and an INPUT statement for the same file is encountered, the pending print record will be written onto the file at the position indicated by the internal counter, and the internal counter is incremented. Then the INPUT statement is performed as usual. If a pending print condition exists and the file is closed or restored, the pending print record is written before the file is closed or restored.

Cassette Recorder Information

- You may specify any record length up to 192 positions.
- You may process SEQUENTIAL files only (you cannot use RELATIVE file-organization with cassette tapes).

RESTORE

RESTORE #*file-number*[,REC *numeric-expression*]

(For a description of the RESTORE statement used with the READ and DATA statements, see "Input-Output Statements.")

The RESTORE statement repositions an open file at its beginning record (see the first example on the right), or at a specific record if the file is RELATIVE (see the second example on the right).

If the *file-number* specified in a RESTORE statement is not already open, the program will terminate with the message "FILE ERROR IN xx."

You may use the REC clause only with a RELATIVE file. The computer evaluates the *numeric-expression* following REC and uses the value as a pointer to a specific record on the file. If you RESTORE a RELATIVE file and do not use the REC clause, the file will be set to record 0.

If there is a pending PRINT record, the record will be written on the file before the RESTORE is performed. If there is a pending INPUT, the data in the I/O buffer is discarded.

RELATIVE files are not supported by cassette recorders.

Examples:

```
>NEW

>100 OPEN #2:"CS1",SEQUENTIAL
,INTERNAL,INPUT,FIXED 64
>110 INPUT #2:A,B,C$,D$,X
 .
 . program lines
 .
>400 RESTORE #2
>410 INPUT #2:A,B,C$,D$,X
 .
 . program lines
 .
>500 CLOSE #2
>510 END
```

```
>NEW

>100 OPEN #4:NAME$,RELATIVE,I
NTERNAL,UPDATE,FIXED 128
>110 INPUT #4:A,B,C
 .
 . program lines
 .
>200 PRINT #4:A,B,C
 .
 . program lines
 .
>300 RESTORE #4,REC 10
>310 INPUT #4:A,B,C
 .
 . program lines
 .
>400 CLOSE #4
>410 END
```

Appendix

ASCII CHARACTER CODES

The defined characters on the TI-99/4A Computer are the standard ASCII characters for codes 32 through 127. The following chart lists these characters and their codes.

ASCII CODE	CHARACTER	ASCII CODE	CHARACTER	ASCII CODE	CHARACTER
32	(space)	65	A	97	A
33	! (exclamation point)	66	B	98	B
34	" (quote)	67	C	99	C
35	# (number or pound sign)	68	D	100	D
36	$ (dollar)	69	E	101	E
37	% (percent)	70	F	102	F
38	& (ampersand)	71	G	103	G
39	' (apostrophe)	72	H	104	H
40	((open parenthesis)	73	I	105	I
41	) (close parenthesis)	74	J	106	J
42	* (asterisk)	75	K	107	K
43	+ (plus)	76	L	108	L
44	, (comma)	77	M	109	M
45	− (minus)	78	N	110	N
46	. (period)	79	O	111	O
47	/ (slant)	80	P	112	P
48	0	81	Q	113	Q
49	1	82	R	114	R
50	2	83	S	115	S
51	3	84	T	116	T
52	4	85	U	117	U
53	5	86	V	118	V
54	6	87	W	119	W
55	7	88	X	120	X
56	8	89	Y	121	Y
57	9	90	Z	122	Z
58	: (colon)	91	[(open bracket)	123	{ (left brace)
59	; (semicolon)	92	\ (reverse slant)	124	¦
60	< (less than)	93	] (close bracket)	125	} (right brace)
61	= (equals)	94	∧ (exponentiation)	126	~ (tilde)
62	> (greater than)	95	_ (line)	127	DEL (appears on screen as a blank.)
63	? (question mark)	96	` (grave)		
64	@ (at sign)				

These character codes are grouped into twelve *sets* for use in color graphics programs.

Set #	Character Codes	Set #	Character Codes	Set #	Character Codes
1	32-39	5	64-71	9	96-103
2	40-47	6	72-79	10	104-111
3	48-55	7	80-87	11	112-119
4	56-63	8	88-95	12	120-127

Two additional characters are predefined on the TI-99/4A Computer. The *cursor* is assigned to ASCII code 30, and the *edge character* is assigned to code 31.

Appendix

FUNCTION AND CONTROL KEY CODES

Codes are also assigned to the function and control keys, so that these can be referenced by the CALL KEY subprogram in TI BASIC. The codes assigned depend on the *key-unit* value specified in a CALL KEY program statement.

Function Key Codes

Codes TI-99/4 & BASIC Modes	Pascal Mode	Function Name	Function Key
1	129	**AID**	FCTN 7
2	130	**CLEAR**	FCTN 4
3	131	**DEL**ete	FCTN 1
4	132	**INS**ert	FCTN 2
5	133	**QUIT**	FCTN =
6	134	**REDO**	FCTN 8
7	135	**ERASE**	FCTN 3
8	136	**LEFT** arrow	FCTN S
9	137	**RIGHT** arrow	FCTN D
10	138	**DOWN** arrow	FCTN X
11	139	**UP** arrow	FCTN E
12	140	**PROD'D**	FCTN 6
13	141	**ENTER**	ENTER
14	142	**BEGIN**	FCTN 5
15	143	**BACK**	FCTN 9

Control Key Codes

Codes BASIC Mode	Pascal Mode	Mnemonic Code	Press	Comments
129	1	SOH	CONTROL A	Start of heading
130	2	STX	CONTROL B	Start of text
131	3	ETX	CONTROL C	End of text
132	4	EOT	CONTROL D	End of transmission
133	5	ENQ	CONTROL E	Enquiry
134	6	ACK	CONTROL F	Acknowledge
135	7	BEL	CONTROL G	Bell
136	8	BS	CONTROL H	Backspace
137	9	HT	CONTROL I	Horizontal tabulation
138	10	LF	CONTROL J	Line feed
139	11	VT	CONTROL K	Vertical tabulation
140	12	FF	CONTROL L	Form feed
141	13	CR	CONTROL M	Carriage return
142	14	SO	CONTROL N	Shift out
143	15	SI	CONTROL O	Shift in
144	16	DLE	CONTROL P	Data link escape
145	17	DC1	CONTROL Q	Device control 1 (X-ON)
146	18	DC2	CONTROL R	Device control 2
147	19	DC3	CONTROL S	Device control 3 (X-OFF)
148	20	DC4	CONTROL T	Device control 4
149	21	NAK	CONTROL U	Negative acknowledge
150	22	SYN	CONTROL V	Synchronous idle
151	23	ETB	CONTROL W	End of transmission block
152	24	CAN	CONTROL X	Cancel
153	25	EM	CONTROL Y	End of medium
154	26	SUB	CONTROL Z	Substitute
155	27	ESC	CONTROL .	Escape
156	28	FS	CONTROL ;	File separator
157	29	GS	CONTROL =	Group separator
158	30	RS	CONTROL 8	Record separator
159	31	US	CONTROL 9	Unit separator

Appendix

KEYBOARD MAPPING

The following diagrams illustrate the key codes returned in the four keyboard modes specified by the *key-unit* value in the CALL KEY statement. The figures on the upper key face are function codes, and the lower figures are control codes.

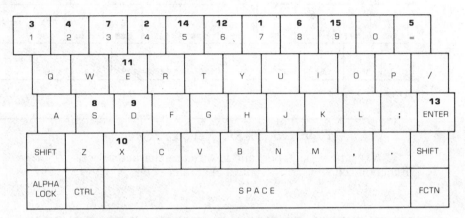

Figure 1. *Standard TI-99/4 Keyboard Scan.*

Key-unit = 3. Both upper- and lower-case alphabetical characters returned as lower-case. Function codes = 1-15. No control characters active.

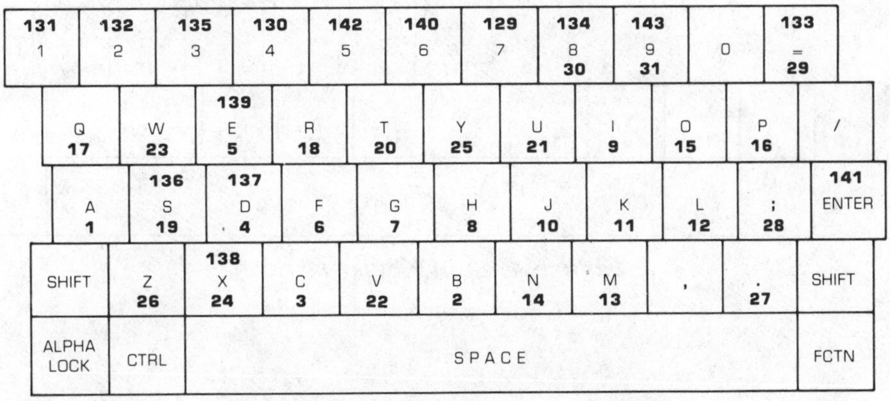

Figure 2. *Pascal Keyboard Scan.*

Key-unit = 4. Upper- and lower-case characters active. Function codes = 129-143. Control character codes = 1-31.

Appendix

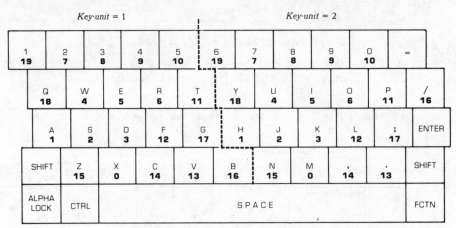

3 1	4 2	7 3	2 4	14 5	12 6	1 7	6 8 158	15 9 159	0	5 = 157

Q 145	W 151	**11** E 133	R 146	T 148	Y 153	U 149	I 137	O 143	P 144	/ 187

A 129	**8** S 147	**9** D 132	F 134	G 135	H 136	J 138	K 139	L 140	; 156	**13** ENTER

SHIFT	Z 154	**10** X 152	C 131	V 150	B 130	N 142	M 141	, 128	. 155	SHIFT

ALPHA LOCK	CTRL	SPACE								FCTN

Figure 3. *BASIC Keyboard Scan.*

Key-unit = 5. Upper- and lower-case characters active.
Function codes = 1-15. Control character codes = 128-159, 187.

Key-unit = 1   Key-unit = 2

1 19	2 7	3 8	4 9	5 10	6 19	7 7	8 8	9 9	0 10	=

Q 18	W 4	E 5	R 6	T 11	Y 18	U 4	I 5	O 6	P 11	/ 16

A 1	S 2	D 3	F 12	G 17	H 1	J 2	K 3	L 12	; 17	ENTER

SHIFT	Z 15	X 0	C 14	V 13	B 16	N 15	M 0	, 14	. 13	SHIFT

ALPHA LOCK	CTRL	SPACE								FCTN

Figure 4. *Split Keyboard Scan.*

Codes returned = 0-19.

CHARACTER CODES FOR SPLIT KEYBOARD

CODES	KEYS*	CODES	KEYS*
0	X,M	10	5,0
1	A,H	11	T,P
2	S,J	12	F,L
3	D,K	13	V, . (period)
4	W,U	14	C, , (comma)
5	E,I	15	Z,N
6	R,0	16	B, / (slash)
7	2,7	17	G, ; (semicolon)
8	3,8	18	Q,Y
9	4,9	19	1,6

*Note that the first key listed is on the left side of the keyboard,
and the second key listed is on the right side of the keyboard.

Appendix

PATTERN-IDENTIFIER CONVERSION TABLE

Blocks	BINARY CODE (0 = off; 1 = on)	HEXADECIMAL CODE
	0000	0
	0001	1
	0010	2
	0011	3
	0100	4
	0101	5
	0110	6
	0111	7
	1000	8
	1001	9
	1010	A
	1011	B
	1100	C
	1101	D
	1110	E
	1111	F

COLOR CODES

COLOR	CODE #	COLOR	CODE #
Transparent	1	Medium Red	9
Black	2	Light Red	10
Medium Green	3	Dark Yellow	11
Light Green	4	Light Yellow	12
Dark Blue	5	Dark Green	13
Light Blue	6	Magenta	14
Dark Red	7	Gray	15
Cyan	8	White	16

Appendix

HIGH-RESOLUTION COLOR COMBINATIONS

The following color combinations produce the sharpest, clearest character resolution on the TI-99/4A color monitor screen. Color codes are included in parentheses.

Black on Medium Green (2, 3)
Black on Light Green (2, 4)
Black on Light Blue (2, 6)
Black on Dark Red (2, 7)
Black on Cyan (2, 8)
Black on Medium Red (2, 9)
Black on Light Red (2, 10)
Black on Dark Yellow (2, 11)
Black on Light Yellow (2, 12)
Black on Dark Green (2, 13)
Black on Magenta (2, 14)
Black on Gray (2, 15)
Black on White (2, 16)
Medium Green on White (3, 16)
Light Green on Black (4, 2)
Light Green on White (4, 16)
Dark Blue on Light Blue (5, 6)
Dark Blue on Gray (5, 15)
Dark Blue on White (5, 16)
Light Blue on Gray (6, 15)
Light Blue on White (6, 16)
Dark Red on Light Yellow (7, 12)
Dark Red on White (7, 16)
Medium Red on Light Red (9, 10)
Medium Red on Light Yellow (9, 12)
Medium Red on White (9, 16)

Light Red on Black (10, 2)
Light Red on Dark Red (10, 7)
Dark Yellow on Black (11, 2)
Light Yellow on Black (12, 2)
Light Yellow on Dark Red (12, 7)
Dark Green on Light Green (13, 4)
Dark Green on Light Yellow (13, 12)
Dark Green on Gray (13, 15)
Dark Green on White (13, 16)
Magenta on Gray (14, 15)
Magenta on White (14, 16)
Gray on Black (15, 2)
Gray on Dark Blue (15, 5)
Gray on Dark Red (15, 7)
Gray on Dark Green (15, 13)
Gray on White (15, 16)
White on Black (16, 2)
White on Medium Green (16, 3)
White on Light Green (16, 4)
White on Dark Blue (16, 5)
White on Light Blue (16, 6)
White on Dark Red (16, 7)
White on Medium Red (16, 9)
White on Light Red (16, 10)
White on Dark Green (16, 13)
White on Magenta (16, 14)
White on Gray (16, 15)

Appendix

MUSICAL TONE FREQUENCIES

The following table gives frequencies (rounded to integers) of four octaves of the tempered scale (one half-step between notes). While this list does not represent the entire range of tones — or even of musical tones — it can be helpful for musical programming.

Frequency	Note	Frequency	Note
110	A	440	A (above middle C)
117	A#,B♭	466	A#,B♭
123	B	494	B
131	C (low C)	523	C (high C)
139	C#,D♭	554	C#,D♭
147	D	587	D
156	D#,E♭	622	D#,E♭
165	E	659	E
175	F	698	F
185	F#,G♭	740	F#,G♭
196	G	784	G
208	G#,A♭	831	G#,A♭
220	A (below middle C)	880	A (above high C)
220	A (below middle C)	880	A (above high C)
233	A#,B♭	932	A#,B♭
247	B	988	B
262	C (middle C)	1047	C
277	C#,D♭	1109	C#,D♭
294	D	1175	D
311	D#,E♭	1245	D#,E♭
330	E	1319	E
349	F	1397	F
370	F#,G♭	1480	F#,G♭
392	G	1568	G
415	G#,A♭	1661	G#,A♭
440	A (above middle C)	1760	A

Error Messages

I. Errors Found When Entering a Line

* **BAD LINE NUMBER**
    1. Line number or line number referenced equals 0 or is greater than 32767
    2. RESEQUENCE specifications generate a line number greater than 32767

* **BAD NAME**
    1. The variable name has more than 15 characters

* **CAN'T CONTINUE**
    1. CONTINUE was entered with no previous breakpoint or program was edited since a breakpoint was taken.

* **CAN'T DO THAT**
    1. Attempting to use the following program statements as commands: DATA, DEF, FOR, GOTO, GOSUB, IF, INPUT, NEXT, ON, OPTION, RETURN
    2. Attempting to use the following commands as program statements (entered with a line number): BYE, CONTINUE, EDIT, LIST, NEW, NUMBER, OLD, RUN, SAVE
    3. Entering LIST, RUN, or SAVE with no program

* **INCORRECT STATEMENT**
    1. Two variable names in a row with no valid separator between them (ABC A or A$A)
    2. A numeric constant immediately follows a variable with no valid separator between them (N 257)
    3. A quoted string has no closing quote mark
    4. Invalid print separator between numbers in the LIST, NUMBER, or RESEQUENCE commands
    5. Invalid characters following CONTINUE, LIST, NUMBER, RESEQUENCE, or RUN commands
    6. Command keyword is not the first word in a line
    7. Colon does not follow the device name in a LIST command

* **LINE TOO LONG**
    1. The input line is too long for the input buffer

* **MEMORY FULL**
    1. Entering an edit line which exceeds available memory
    2. Adding a line to a program causes the program to exceed available memory

II. Errors Found When Symbol Table Is Generated

When RUN is entered but before any program lines are performed, the computer scans the program in order to establish a *symbol table*. A *symbol table* is an area of memory where the variables, arrays, functions, etc., for a program are stored. During this scanning process, the computer recognizes certain errors in the program, as listed below. The number of the line containing the error is printed as part of the message (for example: * BAD VALUE IN 100). Errors in this section are distinguished from those in section III, in that the screen color remains cyan until the symbol table is generated. Since no program lines have been performed at this point, all the values in the *symbol table* will be zero (for numbers) and null (for strings).

* **BAD VALUE**
    1. A dimension for an array is greater than 32767
    2. A dimension for an array is zero when OPTION BASE = 1

* **CAN'T DO THAT**
    1. More than one OPTION BASE statement in your program
    2. The OPTION BASE statement has a higher line number than an array definition

* **FOR-NEXT ERROR**
    1. Mismatched number of FOR and NEXT statements

* **INCORRECT STATEMENT**
    DEF
    1. No closing ")" after a parameter in a DEF statement
    2. Equals sign (=) missing in DEF statement
    3. Parameter in DEF statement is not a valid variable name

Error Messages

DIM
  4. DIM statement has no dimensions or more than three dimensions
  5. A dimension in a DIM statement is not a number
  6. A dimension in a DIM statement is not followed by a comma or a closing ")"
  7. The *array-name* in a DIM statement is not a valid variable name
  8. The closing ")" is missing for array subscripts

OPTION BASE
  9. OPTION not followed by BASE
  10. OPTION BASE not followed by 0 or 1

* **MEMORY FULL**
  1. Array size too large
  2. Not enough memory to allocate a variable or function

* **NAME CONFLICT**
  1. Assigning the same name to more than one array (DIM A(5), A(2,7))
  2. Assigning the same name to an array and a simple variable
  3. Assigning the same name to a variable and a function
  4. References to an array have a different number of dimensions for the array (B=A(2,7)+2, PRINT A(5))

III. Errors Found When a Program Is Running

When a program is running, the computer may encounter statements that it cannot perform. An error message will be printed, and unless the error is only a warning the program will end. At that point, all variables in the program will have the values assigned when the error occurred. The number of the line containing the error will be printed as part of the message (for example: CAN'T DO THAT IN 210).

* **BAD ARGUMENT**
  1. A built-in function has a bad argument
  2. The string expression for the built-in functions ASC or VAL has a zero length (null string)
  3. In the VAL function, the string expression is not a valid representation of a numeric constant

* **BAD LINE NUMBER**
  1. Specified line number does not exist in ON, GOTO or GOSUB statement
  2. Specified line number in BREAK or UNBREAK does not exist (warning only)

* **BAD NAME**
  1. Subprogram name in a CALL statement is invalid

* **BAD SUBSCRIPT**
  1. Subscript is not an integer
  2. Subscript has a value greater than the specified or allowed dimensions of an array
  3. Subscript 0 used when OPTION BASE 1 specified

* **BAD VALUE**

  CHAR
  1. *Character-code* out of range in CHAR statement
  2. Invalid character in *pattern-identifier* in CHAR statement

  CHR$
  3. Argument negative or larger than 32767 in CHR$

  COLOR
  4. *Character-set-number* out of range in COLOR statement
  5. *Foreground* or *background color code* out of range in COLOR statement

  EXPONENTIATION (∧)
  6. Attempting to raise a negative number to a fractional power

  FOR
  7. Step increment is zero in FOR-TO-STEP statement

  HCHAR, VCHAR, GCHAR
  8. *Row* or *column-number* out of range in HCHAR, VCHAR, or GCHAR statement

  JOYST, KEY
  9. *Key-unit* out of range in JOYST or KEY statement

  ON
  10. *Numeric-expression* indexing *line-number* is out of range

Error Messages

OPEN, CLOSE, INPUT, PRINT, RESTORE

11. *File-number* negative or greater than 255
12. Number-of-records in the SEQUENTIAL option of the OPEN statement is non-numeric or greater than 32767
13. *Record-length* in the FIXED option of the OPEN statement is greater than 32767

POS

14. The *numeric-expression* in the POS statement is negative, zero, or larger than 32767

SCREEN

15. Screen *color-code* out of range

SEG$

16. The value of *numeric-expression1* (character position) or *numeric-expression2* (length of substring) is negative or larger than 32767

SOUND

17. *Duration, frequency, volume* or *noise* specification out of range

TAB

18. The value of the character position is greater than 32767 in the TAB function specification

* CAN'T DO THAT

1. RETURN with no previous GOSUB statement
2. NEXT with no previous matching FOR statement
3. The *control-variable* in the NEXT statement does not match the *control-variable* in the previous FOR statement
4. BREAK command with no line number

* DATA ERROR

1. No comma between items in DATA statement
2. *Variable-list* in READ statement not filled but no more DATA statements are available
3. READ statement with no DATA statement remaining

4. Assigning a string value to a numeric variable in a READ statement
5. *Line-number* in RESTORE statement is greater than the highest line number in the program

* FILE ERROR

1. Attempting to CLOSE, INPUT, PRINT, or RESTORE a file not currently open
2. Attempting to INPUT records from a file opened as OUTPUT or APPEND
3. Attempting to PRINT records on a file opened as INPUT
4. Attempting to OPEN a file which is already open

* INCORRECT STATEMENT

General

1. Opening "(", closing ")", or both missing
2. Comma missing
3. No line number where expected in a BREAK, UNBREAK, or RESTORE (BREAK 100,)
4. "+" or "−" not followed by a numeric expression
5. Expressions used with arithmetic operators are not numeric
6. Expressions used with relational operators are not the same type
7. Attempting to use a string expression as a subscript
8. Attempting to assign a value to a function
9. Reserved word out of order
10. Unexpected arithmetic or relational operator is present
11. Expected arithmetic or relational operator missing

Built-in Subprograms

12. In JOYST, the *x-return* and *y-return* are not numeric variables
13. In KEY, the *key-status* is not a numeric variable
14. In GCHAR, the third specification must be a numeric variable
15. More than three tone specifications or more than one noise specification in SOUND
16. CALL is not followed by a subprogram name

Error Messages

File Processing-Input/Output Statements

17. Number sign (#) or colon (:) in *file-number* specification for OPEN, CLOSE, INPUT, PRINT, or RESTORE is missing
18. *File-name* in OPEN or DELETE must be a string expression
19. A keyword in the OPEN statement is invalid or appears more than once
20. The number of records in SEQUENTIAL option is less than zero in the OPEN statement
21. The record length in the FIXED option in the OPEN statement is less than zero or greater than 255
22. A colon (:) in the CLOSE statement is not followed by the keyword DELETE
23. *Print-separator* (comma, colon, semicolon) missing in the PRINT statement where required
24. *Input-prompt* is not a string expression in INPUT statement
25. *File-name* is not a valid string expression in SAVE or OLD command

General Program Statements

FOR

26. The keyword FOR is not followed by a numeric variable
27. In the FOR statement, the *control-variable* is not followed by an equals sign (=)
28. The keyword TO is missing in the FOR statement
29. In the FOR statement, the *limit* is not followed by the end of line or the keyword STEP

IF

30. The keyword THEN is missing or not followed by a line number

LET

31. Equals sign (=) missing in LET statement

NEXT

32. The keyword NEXT is not followed by *control-variable*

ON-GOTO, ON-GOSUB

33. ON is not followed by a valid numeric expression

RETURN

34. Unexpected word or character following the word RETURN

User-Defined Functions

35. The number of function arguments does not match the number of parameters for a user-defined function

* **INPUT ERROR**

1. Input data is too long for Input/Output buffer (if data entered from keyboard, this is only a warning — data can be re-entered)
2. Number of variables in the *variable-list* does not match number of data items input from keyboard or data file (warning only if from keyboard)
3. Non-numeric data INPUT for a numeric variable. This condition could be caused by reading padding characters on a file record. (Warning only if from keyboard)
4. Numeric INPUT data produces an overflow (warning only if from keyboard)

* **I/O ERROR** — This condition generates an accompanying error code as follows:

When an I/O error occurs, a two-digit error code (XY) is displayed with the message:

* I/O ERROR XY IN *line-number*

The first digit (X) indicates which I/O operation caused the error.

X Value	Operation
0	OPEN
1	CLOSE
2	INPUT
3	PRINT
4	RESTORE
5	OLD
6	SAVE
7	DELETE

Error Messages

The second digit (Y) indicates what kind of error occurred.

Y Value	Error Type
0	Device name not found (Invalid device or file name in DELETE, LIST, OLD, or SAVE command)
1	Device write protected (Attempting to write to a protected file)
2	Bad open attribute (One or more OPEN options are illegal or do not match the file characteristics)
3	Illegal operation (Input/output command not valid)
4	Out of space (Attempting to write when insufficient space remains on the storage medium)
5	End of file (Attempting to read past the end of a file)
6	Device error (Device not connected, or is damaged. This error can occur during file processing if an accessory device is accidentally disconnected while the program is running.)
7	File error (The indicated file does not exist or the file type — program file or data file — does not match the access mode.)

* **MEMORY FULL**
1. Not enough memory to allocate the specified character in CHAR statement
2. GOSUB statement branches to its own *line-number*
3. Program contains too many pending subroutine branches with no RETURN performed
4. Program contains too many user-defined functions which refer to other user-defined functions
5. Relational, string, or numeric expression too long
6. User-defined function references itself

* **NUMBER TOO BIG** (warning given — value replaced by computer limit as shown below)
1. A numeric operation produces an overflow (value greater than 9.9999999999999E127 or less than −9.9999999999999E127)
2. READing from DATA statement results in an overflow assignment to a numeric variable
3. INPUT results in an overflow assignment to a numeric variable

* **STRING-NUMBER MISMATCH**
1. A non-numeric argument specified for a built-in function, tab-function, or exponentiation operation
2. A non-numeric value found in a specification requiring a numeric value
3. A non-string value found in a specification requiring a string value
4. Function argument and parameter disagree in type, or function type and expression type disagree for a user-defined function
5. *File-number* not numeric in OPEN, CLOSE, INPUT, PRINT, RESTORE
6. Attempting to assign a string to a numeric variable
7. Attempting to assign a number to a string variable

Note: Additional error codes may occur when you are using various accessories, such as the TI Disk Memory System or Solid State Thermal Printer, with the computer. Consult the appropriate device owner's manual for more information on these error codes.

IV. Error Returned When an OLD Command Is Not Successful

*CHECK PROGRAM IN MEMORY
The OLD command does not clear program memory unless the loading operation is successful. If an OLD command fails or is interrupted, however, any program currently in memory may be partially or completely overwritten by the program being loaded. LIST the program in memory before proceeding.

Accuracy Information

Displayed Results Versus Accuracy

Computers, like all other devices, must operate with a fixed set of rules within preset limits. The TI computer uses especially powerful internal notation to represent numbers.

The mathematical tolerance of the computer is controlled by the number of digits it uses for calculations. The computer appears to use 10 digits as shown by the display, but actually uses more to perform all calculations. When rounded for display purposes, these extra digits help maintain the accuracy of the values presented. Example:

$$\frac{1}{3} \times 3 = .9999999999 \text{ (inaccurate)}$$

The example shows that $\frac{1}{3} = .3333333333$, when multiplied by 3, produces an inaccurate answer. However, a 13-digit string of nines, when rounded to 10 places, will equal 1.0000000000.

The higher order mathematical functions use iterative and polynomial calculations. The cumulative rounding error is usually maintained below the 10-digit display so that no effect can be seen. The 13-digit representation of a number is three orders of magnitude from the displayed tenth digit. In this way the display assures that results are rounded accurately to ten digits.

Normally there is no need to even consider the undisplayed digits. On certain calculations, as with any computer, these digits may appear as an answer when not expected. The mathematical limits of a finite operation (word length, truncation and rounding errors) do not allow these digits to always be completely accurate. Therefore, when subtracting two expressions which are mathematically equal, the computer may display a nonzero result. Example:

$$X = \frac{2}{3} - \frac{1}{3} - \frac{1}{3}$$
$$\text{PRINT X}$$
$$1E-14$$

The final result indicates a discrepancy in the fourteenth digit.

The above fact is especially important when writing your own programs. When testing a calculated result to be equal to another value, precautions should be taken to prevent improper evaluation. For the above example, the statement $X = 1E-10*(INT(X*1E10))$ will truncate the undisplayed digits of the variable X leaving only the rounded display value for further use.

Technical Information on Number Representation

Technically speaking, your computer uses a 7-digit Radix-100 mantissa for internal calculations. A single Radix-100 digit has a range of value from 0 to 99 in base-10 arithmetic. This means that a 7-digit Radix-100 number will correspond to decimal precision of 13 to 14 digits, depending on the value.

Radix-100 exponents range in value from -64 to $+63$ which yield decimal values of 10^{-128} to 10^{+126}. The Radix-100 mantissa and exponent combine to provide an equivalent decimal range of from $-9.9999999999999E127$ through $-1.0000000000000E-128$; zero; and then $+1.0000000000000E-128$ on through $+9.9999999999999E127$.

The internal format of each numerical value consists of eight bytes. The first byte contains the exponent and its sign, biased by 40 hex. The remaining bytes contain the mantissa, with the most significant digit first. The number is normalized so that the decimal point is immediately after the most significant digit. If the number is negative, then the first two bytes are complemented.

Examples:

1. The number 127_{10} is represented as:

EXP	MSD						LSD
41	01	1B	00	00	00	00	00

2. The fraction 0.5_{10} is represented as:

3F	32	00	00	00	00	00	00

3.a) The value of $\pi/2$ is represented as:

40	01	39	07	60	20	43	5F

b) The value of $-\pi/2$ is:

BF	FF	39	07	60	20	43	5F

Applications Programs

Introduction

The programs in this section are designed to illustrate the use of many of the statements in TI BASIC. If you've never had any experience with programming, the best place to begin learning about TI BASIC is the *Beginner's BASIC* book included with your computer. When you've finished reading and working through the programs in that book, these programs will provide additional help in more complex programming. If you've had some experience in programming, these programs will provide a demonstration of many of the TI BASIC features.

The programs included here begin at a simple level and progressively become more complex. Thus, you can begin at whatever level you want. Most of the programs employ the color graphics and sound capabilities of the computer. These should provide you with a good basis for designing your own graphics and adding sound to your programs.

Random Color Dots

This program places random color dots in random locations on the screen. In addition, a random sound is generated and played when the dot is placed on the screen.

The RANDOMIZE statement causes a different sequence of numbers to be generated each time the program is run. The CALL CLEAR statement clears the screen.

This loop assigns each color code (2 through 16) to a different character set (codes 2 through 16).

These statements generate a random musical frequency for the CALL SOUND statement. Statement 170 generates notes from the tempered (twelve-tone) scale.

These statements generate a random character in the range of 40 through 159 and a random row and column location. (The color of the dot depends on the character set of the randomly chosen character.)

These statements produce the sound and place the solid color dot on the screen. Then the program loops back to generate a new sound, color dot, and location.

Examples:

```
>NEW

>100 REM RANDOM COLOR DOTS
>110 RANDOMIZE
>120 CALL CLEAR


>130 FOR C=2 TO 16
>140 CALL COLOR(C,C,C)
>150 NEXT C

>160 N=INT(24*RND)+1
>170 Y=110*(2^(1/12))^N



>180 CHAR=INT(120*RND)+40
>190 ROW=INT(24*RND)+1
>200 COL=INT(32*RND)+1



>210 CALL SOUND(-500,Y,2)
>220 CALL HCHAR(ROW,COL,CHAR)

>230 GOTO 160
>RUN

  -- screen clears

  --random color dots appear
    on the screen at different
    locations
```

(Press **CLEAR** to stop
the program)

Inchworm

This program creates an inchworm that moves back and forth across the screen. When the inchworm reaches the edge of the screen, an "uh-oh" sounds, and the inchworm turns around to go in the opposite direction.

These statements allow you to enter a color for the inchworm (color codes 2-3, 5-16 are recommended). The screen is then cleared. The CALL COLOR statement assigns the color you selected to character set 2. XDIR is used to designate which direction the inchworm moves (+1 indicates right and −1 indicates left).

This loop moves the inchworm across the screen. Line 180 computes where the next block is to be displayed and line 190 places the new block on the screen. The DELAY loop governs how fast the inchworm moves across the screen. Line 220 erases the old color block (so a continuous line won't be drawn) by placing a blank space over the block previously displayed at XOLD. Line 230 saves the current block position so a new one can then be computed. The loop is repeated until the inchworm reaches the edge of the screen.

Line 250 reverses the direction of the inchworm. Lines 260 and 270 produce the "uh-oh" sound. Then line 280 causes the loop to be performed again.

```
>NEW

>100 REM INCHWORM
>110 CALL CLEAR
>120 INPUT "COLOR? ":C
>130 CALL CLEAR
>140 CALL COLOR(2,C,C)
>150 XOLD=1
>160 XDIR=1

>170 FOR I=1 TO 31
>180 XNEW=XOLD+XDIR
>190 CALL HCHAR(12,XNEW,42)
>200 FOR DELAY=1 TO 200
>210 NEXT DELAY
>220 CALL HCHAR(12,XOLD,32)
>230 XOLD=XNEW
>240 NEXT I

>250 XDIR=-XDIR
>260 CALL SOUND(100,392,2)
>270 CALL SOUND(100,330,2)
>280 GOTO 170
>RUN

  --screen clears

  COLOR? 7

  --screen clears

  --inchworm moves back and
    forth across the screen
```

(Press **CLEAR** to stop
the program)

Marquee

This program puts a marquee on the screen. The colors are produced randomly, and a tone sounds each time a color bar is placed on the screen.

These statements clear the screen and assign each character set (2 through 16) to a different color. The RANDOMIZE statement ensures that a different set of colors will be produced each time the program is run.

These statements produce a border for the marquee.

This loop places color bars on the screen moving from left to right (columns 3 through 30). Each time a bar is placed on the screen, a tone sounds. The negative duration allows the sound to be cut off and a new sound to begin each time the CALL SOUND statement is performed. The subroutine beginning at line 310 generates the random colors and tones.

This loop is the same as the loop in lines 200 through 240 except that the color bars are placed on the screen moving from the right to the left. These color bars are placed below those generated by the previous loop. When the loop is finished, the program transfers to line 200 to begin at the left again.

This subroutine generates a random character (thus also generating a random color) for the CALL VCHAR statements (lines 220, 270). The assignment statements in lines 320 and 330 generate a random tone. The RETURN statement transfers the program to the statement following the GOSUB (lines 210, 260).

Examples:

```
>NEW

>100  REM MARQUEE
>110  RANDOMIZE
>120  CALL CLEAR
>130  FOR S=2 TO 16
>140  CALL COLOR(S,S,S)
>150  NEXT S

>160  CALL HCHAR(7,3,64,28)
>170  CALL HCHAR(16,3,64,28)
>180  CALL VCHAR(7,2,64,10)
>190  CALL VCHAR(7,31,64,10)

>200  FOR A=3 TO 30
>210  GOSUB 310
>220  CALL VCHAR(8,A,C,4)
>230  CALL SOUND(-150,Y,2)
>240  NEXT A

>250  FOR A=30 TO 3 STEP -1
>260  GOSUB 310
>270  CALL VCHAR(12,A,C,4)
>280  CALL SOUND(-150,Y,2)
>290  NEXT A
>300  GOTO 200

>310  C=INT(120*RND)+40
>320  N=INT(24*RND)+1
>330  Y=220*(2^(1/12))^N
>340  RETURN
>RUN

  --screen clears

  --marquee appears

(Press CLEAR to stop
 the program)
```

Secret Number

This program is a secret number game. The object is to guess the randomly chosen number between 1 and an upper limit you input. For each guess, you enter two numbers: a low and a high guess. The computer will tell you if the secret number is less than, greater than, or between the two numbers you enter. When you think you know the number, enter the same value for both the low and high guesses.

The RANDOMIZE statement ensures a different sequence of numbers each time the program is run. MSG1$ and MSG2$ are repeatedly used in PRINT statements. The CALL CLEAR statement clears the screen.

The INPUT statement stops the program and waits for you to enter a limit. Then the secret number is generated, and the screen is cleared. N is used to keep track of the number of guesses you make.

This INPUT statement accepts your low and high guesses. If you enter the same number for both guesses and you guess the secret number, the program transfers to line 300. If the secret number is less than your low number, the program transfers to line 260. If the secret number is greater than your high number, the program transfers to line 280. If the secret number is between your two numbers or equal to *one* of your numbers, the program continues.

These statements print a message to tell you where the secret number is in relation to your guesses. Then the program transfers to line 180 to allow you to guess again. If you guessed the secret number, the computer tells you how many guesses you took.

Examples:

```
>NEW

>100 REM SECRET NUMBER
>110 RANDOMIZE
>120 MSG1$="SECRET NUMBER IS"

>130 MSG2$="YOUR TWO NUMBERS"

>140 CALL CLEAR


>150 INPUT "ENTER LIMIT? ":LI
MIT
>160 SECRET=INT(LIMIT*RND)+1
>170 CALL CLEAR
>180 N=N+1


>190 INPUT "LOW,HIGH GUESSES:
 ":LOW,HIGH
>200 IF LOW<>HIGH THEN 220
>210 IF SECRET=LOW THEN 300
>220 IF SECRET<LOW THEN 260
>230 IF SECRET>HIGH THEN 280


>240 PRINT MSG1$&" BETWEEN":M
SG2$
>250 GOTO 180
>260 PRINT MSG1$&" LESS THAN"
:MSG2$
>270 GOTO 180
>280 PRINT MSG1$&" LARGER THA
N":MSG2$
>290 GOTO 180
>300 PRINT "YOU GUESSED THE S
ECRET"
>310 PRINT "NUMBER IN ";N;"TR
IES"
```

Secret Number

These statements offer you the choice of playing again or stopping the program. If you enter any character other than Y, the program ends. If you wish to play again, the counter for the number of guesses is set to zero, and you are asked if you want to set a new limit. If you enter Y, the program transfers back to line 140. If you enter any other character, the program transfers to line 160 to generate a new secret number.

Here is a sample of the program run. (Of course, your secret numbers will be different from the one shown here.)

Examples:

```
>320 PRINT "WANT TO PLAY AGAI
N?"
>330 INPUT "ENTER Y OR N: ":A
$
>340 IF A$<>"Y" THEN 390
>350 N=0
>360 PRINT "WANT TO SET A NEW
 LIMIT?"
>370 INPUT "ENTER Y OR N: ":B
$
>380 IF B$="Y" THEN 140 ELSE
160
>390 END


>RUN

 --screen clears

 ENTER LIMIT? 20

 --screen clears

 LOW,HIGH GUESSES: 1,10
 SECRET NUMBER IS BETWEEN
 YOUR TWO NUMBERS

 LOW,HIGH GUESSES: 1,5
 SECRET NUMBER IS LARGER THAN
 YOUR TWO NUMBERS

 LOW,HIGH GUESSES: 7,7
 YOU GUESSED THE SECRET
 NUMBER IN  3 TRIES
 WANT TO PLAY AGAIN?
 ENTER Y OR N: N

 ** DONE **
```

Bouncing Ball

This program moves a ball and bounces it off the edges of the screen. Each time the ball hits any side, a tone sounds, and the ball is deflected. The following special character is used to define the ball.

			X	X	X			*Block Codes*
		X	X	X	X	X		3C
		X	X	X	X	X	X	7E
	X	X	X	X	X	X	X	FF
	X	X	X	X	X	X	X	FF
	X	X	X	X	X	X	X	FF
	X	X	X	X	X	X	X	FF
		X	X	X	X	X		7E
			X	X	X			3C

These statements clear the screen and define character 96 as the ball.

These statements allow you to input the color of the ball and the screen background color. Note that defining the screen color by using character set 1, which includes character 32 (the blank space), gives definite limits for the screen edge. The screen is cleared when the colors have been entered.

These statements give the starting position for the ball and set the parameters which will control the X and Y direction.

These statements compute the next ball position. The direction the ball moves depends on the current values of XDIR (+1 indicates right, −1 indicates left) and YDIR (+1 indicates up, −1 indicates down).

These statements test to see if the new ball position is still on the screen. If either the row (Y) or column (X) value is out of range, then the program transfers to line 310 (column out of range) or line 360 (row out of range) to change the ball direction.

Examples:

```
>NEW

>100 REM BOUNCING BALL
>110 CALL CLEAR
>120 CALL CHAR(96,"3C7EFFFFFF
  FF7E3C")


>130 INPUT "BALL COLOR? ":C
>140 INPUT "SCREEN COLOR? ":S

>150 CALL CLEAR
>160 CALL COLOR(9,C,S)
>170 CALL COLOR(1,S,S)

>180 X=16
>190 Y=12
>200 XDIR=1
>210 YDIR=1


>220 X=X+XDIR
>230 Y=Y+YDIR


>240 IF X<1 THEN 310
>250 IF X>32 THEN 310
>260 IF Y<1 THEN 360
>270 IF Y>24 THEN 360
```

Bouncing Ball

If the new ball position is still on the screen, then the screen is cleared to erase the old ball location. The ball is then displayed at the new location designated by Y and X.

These statements change the direction of the ball if X is out of range. The CALL SOUND statement produces the "bouncing" tone. Lines 330 and 340 check to see if Y is also out of range. If it is, the program transfers to change the Y direction. If not, the program transfers to line 220 to compute a new ball position.

These statements change the direction of the ball if Y is out of range. The CALL SOUND statement produces the "bouncing" tone. The program then transfers to line 220 to compute the new ball position.

Examples:

```
>280 CALL CLEAR
>290 CALL HCHAR(Y,X,96)
>300 GOTO 220


>310 XDIR=-XDIR
>320 CALL SOUND(30,380,2)
>330 IF Y<1 THEN 360
>340 IF Y>24 THEN 360
>350 GOTO 220


>360 YDIR=-YDIR
>370 CALL SOUND(30,380,2)
>380 GOTO 220
>RUN

  --screen clears

BALL COLOR? 5
SCREEN COLOR? 15

  --ball appears in center of
    screen and begins bouncing
```

(Press **CLEAR** to stop
the program)

Checkbook Balance

Once each month all of us have the opportunity to tackle "balancing" our checkbooks against our bank statements. Normally, the checkbook balance will not agree with the balance shown on the bank statement because there are checks and deposits that haven't cleared yet. This program will help you balance your checkbook quickly and easily.

These statements clear the screen and allow you to input the balance shown on your bank statement.

These statements give instructions for entering your outstanding check numbers and amounts. Note that DISPLAY and PRINT can be used interchangeably.

This loop sets up the procedure for entering each check number and amount. These values are stored in arrays. If the check number equals zero, the program transfers out of the loop. CTOTAL is the total amount of outstanding checks. Each time a check amount is input, the program transfers to line 190 to input another check number and amount.

These statements give instructions for entering your outstanding deposits.

This loop asks for and accepts each outstanding deposit amount. If the deposit amount equals zero, the program transfers out of the loop. DTOTAL is the total amount of outstanding deposits. After each outstanding deposit is added to the total, the program transfers to line 310 to accept another deposit amount.

Examples:

```
>NEW

>100 REM CHECKBOOK BALANCE
>110 CALL CLEAR
>120 INPUT "BANK BALANCE? ":B
ALANCE

>130 DISPLAY "ENTER EACH OUTS
ANDING"
>140 DISPLAY "CHECK NUMBER AN
D AMOUNT."
>150 DISPLAY
>160 DISPLAY "ENTER A ZERO FO
R THE"
>170 DISPLAY "CHECK NUMBER WH
EN FINISHED."
>180 DISPLAY

>190 N=N+1
>200 INPUT "CHECK NUMBER? ":C
NUM(N)
>210 IF CNUM(N)=0 THEN 250
>220 INPUT "CHECK AMOUNT? ":C
AMT(N)
>230 CTOTAL=CTOTAL+CAMT(N)
>240 GOTO 190

>250 DISPLAY "ENTER EACH OUTS
TANDING"
>260 DISPLAY "DEPOSIT AMOUNT.
"
>270 DISPLAY
>280 DISPLAY "ENTER A ZERO AM
OUNT"
>290 DISPLAY "WHEN FINISHED."

>300 DISPLAY

>310 M=M+1
>320 INPUT "DEPOSIT AMOUNT? "
:DAMT(M)
>330 IF DAMT(M)=0 THEN 360
>340 DTOTAL=DTOTAL+DAMT(M)
>350 GOTO 310
```

Checkbook Balance

These statements compute and display the new balance. Then you enter the current balance in your checkbook. (Be sure you have subtracted bank service charges before you enter the current balance.) The correction necessary to make your checkbook agree with the bank statement is then computed and displayed.

Here is a sample program run.

Examples:

```
>360 NBAL=BALANCE-CTOTAL+DTOT
AL
>370 DISPLAY "NEW BALANCE= ";
NBAL
>380 INPUT "CHECKBOOK BALANCE
? ":CBAL
>390 DISPLAY "CORRECTION= ";N
BAL-CBAL
>400 END


>RUN

 --screen clears

 BANK BALANCE? 940.26

 ENTER EACH OUTSTANDING
 CHECK NUMBER AND AMOUNT.

 ENTER A ZERO FOR THE
 CHECK NUMBER WHEN FINISHED.

 CHECK NUMBER? 212
 CHECK AMOUNT? 76.83
 CHECK NUMBER? 213
 CHECK AMOUNT? 122.87
 CHECK NUMBER? 216
 CHECK AMOUNT? 219.50
 CHECK NUMBER? 218
 CHECK AMOUNT? 397.31
 CHECK NUMBER? 219
 CHECK AMOUNT? 231.00
 CHECK NUMBER? 220
 CHECK AMOUNT? 138.25
 CHECK NUMBER? 0
 ENTER EACH OUTSTANDING
 DEPOSIT AMOUNT.

 ENTER A ZERO AMOUNT
 WHEN FINISHED.

 DEPOSIT AMOUNT? 450
 DEPOSIT AMOUNT? 0
 NEW BALANCE=  204.5

 CHECKBOOK BALANCE? 209.15
 CORRECTION= -4.65

 ** DONE **
```

Codebreaker

Codebreaker is a game in which the computer generates a four-digit code number, and you try to guess it. Zeros are not allowed, and no two digits may be the same. Even with these restrictions, there are 3024 possible codes, making slim your chances of guessing the number on the first try. Your guess is automatically scored by the computer. Your score for each guess is displayed in the form "N.R," where N is the number of digits in your trial number that appear in the secret number and are positioned correctly and R is the number of digits in your guess which although correct, are improperly placed. For example, if the number generated by the computer is 8261 and you guess 6285, you receive a score of 1.2. This indicates that one number you guessed is in the right place (the 2) and that two of your other numbers (8 and 6) are present in the secret number, but not in the right place. A score of 4.0 indicates that your guess is correct.

The RANDOMIZE statement ensures that a different number will be generated each time the program is run. After the screen is cleared, the computer generates the four-digit number. Note that each digit is stored separately in the array, N. The J-loop beginning at line 160 ensures that no two digits in the number generated are the same. The number of tries is set to zero for each new four-digit number generated.

The INPUT statement stops the program and waits for you to enter your guess. Be sure to enter a four-digit integer number. Each time you guess a number, the score is set to zero, and the number of tries is increased by one.

Line 250 takes the last digit from the guess so that it may be compared against the code number. If the digit matches the code number in the same position, then the score is increased by 1. If not, then the L-loop is used to compare the digit against the other positions in the code number. If it matches any other position in the code number, then .1 is added to the score. Line 340 eliminates the last digit from the guess, so that the next digit can be taken for the comparison. When all four digits have been compared, the program continues at line 360.

Examples:

```
>NEW

>100 REM CODEBREAKER GAME
>110 RANDOMIZE
>120 CALL CLEAR
>130 FOR I=1 TO 4
>140 N(I)=INT(9*RND)+1
>150 IF I=1 THEN 190
>160 FOR J=1 TO I-1
>170 IF N(I)=N(J) THEN 140
>180 NEXT J
>190 NEXT I
>200 TRIES=0

>210 INPUT "ENTER GUESS? ":GU
ESS
>220 SCORE=0
>230 TRIES=TRIES+1

>240 FOR K=4 TO 1 STEP -1
>250 DIGIT=(GUESS/10-INT(GUES
S/10))*10
>260 IF DIGIT<>N(K) THEN 290
>270 SCORE=SCORE+1
>280 GOTO 340
>290 FOR L=1 TO 4
>300 IF N(L)<>DIGIT THEN 330
>310 SCORE=SCORE+.1
>320 GOTO 340
>330 NEXT L
>340 GUESS=INT(GUESS/10)
>350 NEXT K
```

Codebreaker

These statements print the score for each guess. Strings are used in displaying the score to insure that the score is always displayed in the "N.R " format. If the score is an integer number, then a ".0" (line 370) must be added after the number. If the score is less than one, then a "0" (line 400) must be added before the number. If the score is a non-integer and greater than one, then just the score itself is printed (line 420). If the score is not equal to 4, the program transfers to line 210 to accept another guess.

These statements print the number of tries you took to guess the code number. Then the computer asks if you want to play again. If you enter Y, the program transfers to line 110 to generate a new number. If you enter anything else, the program stops.

Here is a sample of a program run. (Of course, your code numbers will be different.)

Character Definition

This program allows you to define special graphics characters using the computer. An 8×8 grid is displayed on the screen. You then choose which "dots" to turn *on* and which to leave turned *off*. After the character has been designed, the program determines and displays the HEX string to be entered in the CALL CHAR statement.

These statements define the *off* dot character (line 120) and the *on* dot character (line 130). Black is used as the foreground color (*on* dot) and white is used as the background color (*off* dot). The screen is then cleared and the labels needed on the screen are displayed at the necessary locations. Note that the subroutine beginning at line 770 is used to print a string horizontally on the screen and the subroutine beginning at line 820 is used to print a string vertically on the screen. The R-loop is used to place the 8×8 grid (all dots turned *off*) on the screen.

This loop allows you to turn the "dots" either *on* or *off*. To turn a dot *on*, press the 1 key. To leave a dot turned *off*, press the 0 key. The cursor starts in the upper left corner (row 1, column 1) of the grid. Each time you press a key, the dot is turned *on* or *off* and the cursor moves to the next position. When the end of a row is reached, the cursor automatically moves to the next row. When the last "dot" is turned *on* or *off*, the program continues to determine the HEX string. Line 430 performs a logical OR. If the key you pressed was not a zero or a one, the program transfers back to line 370 to accept a new key input. Errors in the grid can be corrected before the last dot (row 8, column 8) is entered by using the LEFT arrow and RIGHT arrow keys. If either of these keys is pressed, then the program transfers to the subroutine beginning at line 870. The subroutine moves the cursor in the appropriate direction and to the next row up or down as necessary.

These statements determine the hexadecimal code for each row in the grid. When the code is determined, character 102 is defined to be the character shown on the large grid. The newly defined character is then displayed on the screen at row 8, column 20. The character is also displayed in a 3-by-3 pattern. Then the hexadecimal code defining that character is displayed. Lines 630 through 720 print instructions on the screen for you to define a new character. If you are finished defining characters, press Q and the program stops. If you press any other key, the program transfers to line 140 to clear the screen and begin again.

Examples:

```
>NEW

>100 REM CHARACTER DEFINITION

>110 DIM B(8,8)
>120 CALL CHAR(100,"")
>130 CALL CHAR(101,"FFFFFFFF
     FFFFFFFF")
>140 CALL COLOR(9,2,16)
>150 CALL CLEAR
>160 M$="AUTO CHARACTER DEFIN
     ITION"
>170 Y=3
>180 X=4
>190 GOSUB 770
>200 M$="12345678"
>210 Y=8
>220 GOSUB 770
>230 GOSUB 820
>240 M$="0=OFF=WHITE"
>250 Y=22
>260 X=4
>270 GOSUB 770
>280 M$="1=ON=BLACK"
>290 Y=23
>300 GOSUB 770
>310 FOR R=1 TO 8
>320 CALL HCHAR(8+R,5,100,8)
>330 NEXT R
>340 FOR R=1 TO 8
>350 FOR C=1 TO 8
>360 CALL HCHAR(8+R,4+C,30)
>370 CALL KEY(0,KEY,STATUS)
>380 IF STATUS=0 THEN 370
>390 IF (KEY<>8)+(KEY<>9)=-2
     THEN 420
>400 GOSUB 870
>410 GOTO 360
>420 KEY=KEY-48
>430 IF (KEY<0)+(KEY>1)<=-1 T
     HEN 370
>440 B(R,C)=KEY
>450 CALL HCHAR(8+R,4+C,100+K
     EY)
>460 NEXT C
>470 NEXT R

>480 HEX$="0123456789ABCDEF"
>490 M$=""
>500 FOR R=1 TO 8
>510 LOW=B(R,5)*8+B(R,6)*4+B(
     R,7)*2+B(R,8)+1
>520 HIGH=B(R,1)*8+B(R,2)*4+B
     (R,3)*2+B(R,4)+1
>530 M$=M$&SEG$(HEX$,HIGH,1)&
     SEG$(HEX$,LOW,1)
>540 NEXT R
>550 CALL CHAR(102,M$)
>560 CALL HCHAR(8,20,102)
>570 FOR R=0 TO 2
>580 CALL HCHAR(12+R,20,102,3
     )
>590 NEXT R
```

Character Definition

Examples:

```
>600 Y=16
>610 X=12
>620 GOSUB 770
>630 M$="PRESS Q TO QUIT"
>640 Y=18
>650 X=12
>660 GOSUB 770
>670 M$="PRESS ANY OTHER"
>680 Y=19
>690 GOSUB 770
>700 M$="KEY TO CONTINUE"
>710 Y=20
>720 GOSUB 770
>730 CALL KEY(0,KEY,STATUS)
>740 IF STATUS=0 THEN 730
>750 IF KEY<>81 THEN 140
>760 STOP
>770 FOR I=1 TO LEN(M$)
>780 CODE=ASC(SEG$(M$,I,1))
>790 CALL HCHAR(Y,X+I,CODE)
>800 NEXT I
>810 RETURN
>820 FOR I=1 TO LEN(M$)
>830 CODE=ASC(SEG$(M$,I,1))
>840 CALL HCHAR(Y+I,X,CODE)
>850 NEXT I
>860 RETURN
>870 CALL HCHAR(8+R,4+C,100+B
 (R,C))
>880 IF KEY=9 THEN 960
>890 C=C-1
>900 IF C<>0 THEN 1020
>910 C=8
>920 R=R-1
>930 IF R<>0 THEN 1020
>940 R=8
>950 GOTO 1020
>960 C=C+1
>970 IF C<>9 THEN 1020
>980 C=1
>990 R=R+1
>1000 IF R<>9 THEN 1020
>1010 R=1
>1020 RETURN
>RUN

--screen clears
```
```

These subroutines print a given string beginning at a specified row and column on the screen. Lines 770 through 810 print a string horizontally. Lines 820 through 860 print a string vertically.

This subroutine is used to allow you to change the dots you have turned *on* or *off*. First, the new cursor location is checked. If the cursor is at the end of the line and the RIGHT arrow key is pressed, the cursor moves to the left side of the next line down. If the cursor is at the beginning of the line and the LEFT arrow key is pressed, the cursor moves to the right side of the next line up. If the cursor is at the upper left corner and the LEFT arrow key is pressed, the cursor moves to the lower right corner. If the cursor is at the lower right corner and the RIGHT arrow key is pressed, the cursor moves to the upper left hand corner.

A sample of the screen for a program run is shown at the right.

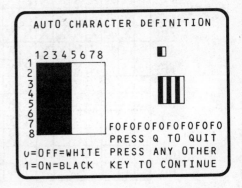
```

Graphics Match

This game program gives an example of developing special graphics for your own use. There are six different graphics characters defined. These are: heart, cherry, bell, lemon, diamond, and bar. To play the game you need only to run the program. The computer generates three random numbers in the range 1 through 6. Each time a number is generated, the picture corresponding to the number is displayed on the screen. Scoring depends on how many and in what way the three pictures match. When the three pictures and the score have been displayed, you are offered the choice of playing again.

These statements define the colors for each of the characters. The colors used are:

Graphics Character	Color
Heart	Medium Red
Cherry	Medium Red with Dark Green stem
Bell	Light Blue with Black handle
Lemon	Dark Yellow
Diamond	Dark Green
Bar	Dark Blue

A white background is used for all of the pictures.

These statements define the heart.

Examples:

>NEW

>100 REM GRAPHICS MATCH
>110 CALL COLOR(9,7,16)
>120 CALL COLOR(10,13,16)
>130 CALL COLOR(11,2,16)
>140 CALL COLOR(12,6,16)
>150 CALL COLOR(13,11,16)
>160 CALL COLOR(14,5,16)

>170 CALL CHAR(96,"00001C3E7F 7F7F7F")
>180 CALL CHAR(97,"0000387CFE FEFEFE")
>190 CALL CHAR(98,"3F1F0F0703 01")
>200 CALL CHAR(99,"FCF8F0E0C0 80")

Block Codes		Block Codes
00		00
00		00
1C		38
3E		7C
7F		FE
7F		FE
7F		FE
7F		FE
3F		FC
1F		F8
0F		F0
07		E0
03		C0
01		80
00		00
00		00

Graphics Match

Note that in lines 190 and 200, the last four zeros are omitted. This saves time in entering the lines since the computer automatically fills the remaining length of the string with zeros.

These statements define the cherry.

Block Codes		Block Codes
00		00
00		00
00	(grid)	06
00		08
00		10
1F		20
3F		40
7F		80
7F		E0
7F		F0
7F		F0
7F		F0
3F		F0
3F		E0
1F		C0
00		00

These statements define the bell.

Block Codes		Block Codes
00		00
00		00
01	(grid)	80
01		80
01		80
01		80
01		80
01		80
03		C0
07		E0
07		E0
07		E0
07		E0
0F		E0
07		E0
01		80

Examples:

>210 CALL CHAR(100,"000000000
  01F3F7F")
>220 CALL CHAR(104,"000006081
  0204080")
>230 CALL CHAR(101,"7F7F7F7F3
  F3F1F")
>240 CALL CHAR(102,"E0F0F0F0F
  0E0C0")

>250 CALL CHAR(112,"000001010
  1010101")
>260 CALL CHAR(113,"000080808
  0808080")
>270 CALL CHAR(120,"030707070
  70F0701")
>280 CALL CHAR(121,"C0E0E0E0E
  0F0E080")

Graphics Match

These statements define the lemon.

Examples:

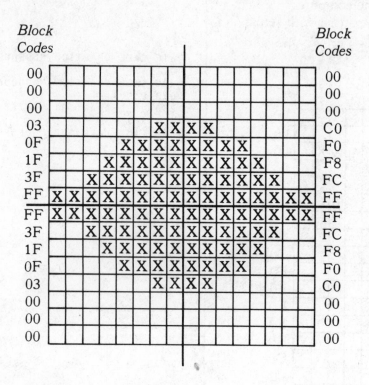

Block Codes	Block Codes
00	00
00	00
00	00
03	C0
0F	F0
1F	F8
3F	FC
FF	FF
FF	FF
3F	FC
1F	F8
0F	F0
03	C0
00	00
00	00
00	00

```
>290 CALL CHAR(128,"000000030
 F1F3FFF")
>300 CALL CHAR(129,"000000C0F
 0F8FCFF")
>310 CALL CHAR(130,"FF3F1F0F0
 3")
>320 CALL CHAR(131,"FFFCF8F0C
 0")
```

These statements define the diamond.

Block Codes	Block Codes
00	00
01	80
03	C0
07	E0
0F	F0
1F	F8
3F	FC
7F	FE
7F	FE
3F	FC
1F	F8
0F	F0
07	E0
03	C0
01	80
00	00

```
>330 CALL CHAR(105,"000103070
 F1F3F7F")
>340 CALL CHAR(106,"0080C0E0F
 0F8FCFE")
>350 CALL CHAR(107,"7F3F1F0F0
 70301")
>360 CALL CHAR(108,"FEFCF8F0E
 0C080")
```

Graphics Match

These statements define the bar.

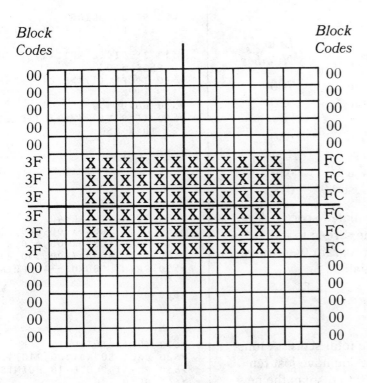

Examples:

```
>370 CALL CHAR(136,"000000000
     03F3F3F")
>380 CALL CHAR(137,"000000000
     0FCFCFC")
>390 CALL CHAR(138,"3F3F3F")
>400 CALL CHAR(139,"FCFCFC")
```

The RANDOMIZE statement insures that a different sequence of pictures is generated each time the program is run. The variable C indicates the starting column location for the next picture. The I-loop generates a random number between 1 and 6, inclusive. The ON-GOSUB statement (line 460) transfers the program to the appropriate subroutine to place the picture on the screen. The pictures are displayed according to the following values:

```
>410 RANDOMIZE
>420 CALL CLEAR
>430 C=14
>440 FOR I=1 TO 3
>450 PIC(I)=INT(6*RND)+1
>460 ON PIC(I) GOSUB 840,900,
     960,1020,1080,1140
>470 C=C+2
>480 NEXT I
```

PIC(I)	Picture
1	Heart
2	Cherry
3	Bell
4	Lemon
5	Diamond
6	Bar

After the picture is placed on the screen, the program returns to the loop to generate a new number and picture. When three pictures are displayed, the program continues to score the results.

Graphics Match

These statements determine the score you receive, as outlined in the table below. The line number indicates the line to which the program transfers to award the points.

Match	Points	Line Number
All pictures alike	Win 75	700
First two pictures, a cherry, lemon, or bar	Win 40	550
First two pictures a heart, bell, or diamond	Win 10	650
First and last pictures alike	Win 10	650
No match or last two pictures alike	Lose 10	610

These statements add 40 points to the accumulated score. Three tones sound and a message is displayed on the screen to indicate you have won a bonus worth 40 points. The program then transfers to line 770 to display the total points accumulated.

In line 610, ten points are subtracted from the total score. A tone sounds and a message is displayed to indicate you have lost ten points. The program then transfers to line 770 to display the new score.

In these statements, ten points are added to the total score. To indicate that you have won ten points, two tones sound and a message is displayed. Then the program transfers to line 770 to display the new score.

These statements add 75 points to the total score. Five tones sound and a message indicating that you have won the jackpot is displayed.

The PRINT statement in line 770 prints your current score. The other statements offer you the choice of playing again or stopping the program. The CALL KEY statement (line 800) accepts an answer without your having to press **ENTER.** Pressing the **Y** key instructs the program to transfer back to line 410 to generate three new pictures. Pressing any other key stops the program.

Examples:

```
>490 REM SCORING
>500 IF PIC(1)<>PIC(2) THEN 5
20
>510 IF PIC(2)=PIC(3) THEN 70
0 ELSE 540
>520 IF PIC(1)<>PIC(3) THEN 6
10
>530 GOTO 650
>540 IF PIC(1)/2<>INT(PIC(1)/
2) THEN 650

>550 TOTAL=TOTAL+40
>560 CALL SOUND(100,440,2)
>570 CALL SOUND(100,660,2)
>580 CALL SOUND(100,550,2)
>590 PRINT "BONUS--40 POINTS"

>600 GOTO 770

>610 TOTAL=TOTAL-10
>620 CALL SOUND(100,110,1)
>630 PRINT "LOSE 10 POINTS"
>640 GOTO 770

>650 TOTAL=TOTAL+10
>660 CALL SOUND(100,660,2)
>670 CALL SOUND(100,770,2)
>680 PRINT "WIN 10 POINTS"
>690 GOTO 770

>700 TOTAL=TOTAL+75
>710 CALL SOUND(100,440,2)
>720 CALL SOUND(100,550,2)
>730 CALL SOUND(100,440,2)
>740 CALL SOUND(100,660,2)
>750 CALL SOUND(100,880,2)
>760 PRINT "JACKPOT!--75 POIN
TS"

>770 PRINT "CURRENT TOTAL POI
NTS: ";TOTAL
>780 PRINT "WANT TO PLAY AGAI
N?"
>790 PRINT "PRESS Y FOR YES"
>800 CALL KEY(0,KEY,STATUS)
>810 IF STATUS=0 THEN 800
>820 IF KEY=89 THEN 410
>830 END
```

Graphics Match

These six subroutines print each of the six pictures. The RETURN statements are used so that only one picture will be printed for each call to a subroutine.

Examples:

```
>840 REM PRINT HEART
>850 CALL HCHAR(12,C,96)
>860 CALL HCHAR(12,C+1,97)
>870 CALL HCHAR(13,C,98)
>880 CALL HCHAR(13,C+1,99)
>890 RETURN
>900 REM PRINT CHERRY
>910 CALL HCHAR(12,C,100)
>920 CALL HCHAR(12,C+1,104)
>930 CALL HCHAR(13,C,101)
>940 CALL HCHAR(13,C+1,102)
>950 RETURN
>960 REM PRINT BELL
>970 CALL HCHAR(12,C,112)
>980 CALL HCHAR(12,C+1,113)
>990 CALL HCHAR(13,C,120)
>1000 CALL HCHAR(13,C+1,121)
>1010 RETURN
>1020 REM PRINT LEMON
>1030 CALL HCHAR(12,C,128)
>1040 CALL HCHAR(12,C+1,129)
>1050 CALL HCHAR(13,C,130)
>1060 CALL HCHAR(13,C+1,131)
>1070 RETURN
>1080 REM PRINT DIAMOND
>1090 CALL HCHAR(12,C,105)
>1100 CALL HCHAR(12,C+1,106)
>1110 CALL HCHAR(13,C,107)
>1120 CALL HCHAR(13,C+1,108)
>1130 RETURN
>1140 REM PRINT BAR
>1150 CALL HCHAR(12,C,136)
>1160 CALL HCHAR(12,C+1,137)
>1170 CALL HCHAR(13,C,138)
>1180 CALL HCHAR(13,C+1,139)
>1190 RETURN
```

Graphics Match

Here is a sample program run. Note that the computer screen remains cyan while the computer generates the symbol table and scans the program for errors. This takes about a minute.

Examples:

```
>RUN
```

--screen clears

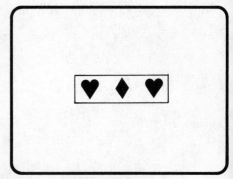

--two tones sound

```
♥ ♦ ♥

WIN 10 POINTS
CURRENT TOTAL POINTS: 10
WANT TO PLAY AGAIN?
PRESS Y FOR YES
```

PRESS Y FOR YES

** DONE **

Glossary

Accessory devices — additional equipment which attaches to the computer and extends its functions and capabilities. Included are preprogrammed *Command Modules** and units which send, receive or store computer data, such as printers and disks. These are often called peripherals.

Array — a collection of numeric or string variables, arranged in a list or matrix for processing by the computer. Each element in an array is referenced by a *subscript** describing its position in the list.

ASCII — the American Standard Code for Information Interchange, the code structure used internally in most personal computers to represent letters, numbers, and special characters.

BASIC — an easy-to-use popular programming language used in most personal computers. The word BASIC is an acronym for "Beginners All-purpose Symbolic Instruction Code."

Baud — commonly used to refer to bits per second.

Binary — a number system based on two digits, 0 and 1. The internal language and operations of the computer are based on the binary system.

Branch — a departure from the sequential performance of program statements. An unconditional branch causes the computer to jump to a specified program line every time the branching statement is encountered. A conditional branch transfers program control based on the result of some arithmetic or logical operation.

Breakpoint — a point in the program specified by the BREAK command where program execution can be suspended. During a breakpoint, you can perform operations in the *Command Mode** to help you locate program errors. Program execution can be resumed with a CONTINUE command, unless editing took place while the program was stopped.

Buffer — an area of computer memory for temporary storage of an input or output record.

Bug — a hardware defect or programming error which causes the intended operation to be performed incorrectly.

Byte — a string of *binary** digits (bits) treated as a unit, often representing one data *character**. The computer's memory capacity is often expressed as the number of bytes available. For example, a computer with 16K bytes of memory has about 16,000 bytes available for storing programs and data.

Character — a letter, number, punctuation symbol, or special graphics symbol.

Command — an instruction which the computer performs immediately. Commands are not a part of a program and thus are entered with no preceding line number.

Command Mode — when no program is running, the computer is in the Command (or Immediate) Mode and performs each task as it is entered.

Command Modules — preprogrammed *ROM** modules which are easily inserted in the TI computer to extend its capabilities.

Concatenation — linking two or more *strings** to make a longer string. The "&" is the concatenation operator.

Constant — a specific numeric or *string** value. A numeric constant is any real number, such as 1.2 or −9054. A string constant is any combination of up to 112 characters enclosed in quotes, such as "HELLO THERE" or "275 FIRST ST."

Cursor — a symbol which indicates where the next *character** will appear on the screen when you press a key.

Data — basic elements of information which are processed or produced by the computer.

Default — a standard characteristic or value which the computer assumes if certain specifications are omitted within a *statement** or a *program**.

Device (see *Accessory Devices*)

Disk — a mass storage device capable of random and sequential access.

*See definition in *Glossary*.

Glossary

Display — (noun) the video screen; (verb) to cause characters to appear on the screen.

Edit Mode — the mode used to change existing program lines. The EDIT mode is entered by using the Edit Command or by entering the line number followed by **SHIFT** ⬇ or **SHIFT** ⬆. The line specified is displayed on the screen and changes can be made to any *character** using the editing keys.

End-of-file — the condition indicating that all *data** has been read from a *file**.

Execute — to run a program; to perform the task specified by a *statement** or *command**.

Exponent — a number indicating the power to which a number or *expression** is to be raised; usually written at the right and above the number. For example, $2^8 = 2 \times 2 \times 2 \times 2 \times 2 \times 2 \times 2 \times 2$. In TI BASIC the exponent is entered following the ∧ symbol or following the letter "E" in *scientific notation**. For example, $2^8 = 2 \wedge 8$; $1.3 \times 10^{25} = 1.3E25$.

Expression — a combination of constants, variables, and operators which can be evaluated to a single result. Included are numeric, string, and relational expressions.

File — a collection of related data records stored on a device; also used interchangeably with *device** for input/output equipment which cannot use multiple files, such as a line printer.

Fixed-length records — records in a *file** which are all the same length. If a file has fixed-length records of 95 characters, each record will be allocated 95 *bytes** even if the *data** occupies only 76 positions. The computer will add padding characters on the right to ensure that the record has the specified length.

Function — a feature which allows you to specify as "single" operations a variety of procedures, each of which actually contains a number of steps; for example, a procedure to produce the square root via a simple reference name.

Graphics — visual constructions on the screen, such as graphs, patterns, and drawings, both stationary and animated. TI BASIC has built-in subprograms which provide easy-to-use color graphic capabilities.

Graphics line — a 32-character line used by the TI BASIC graphics subprograms.

Hardware — the various devices which comprise a computer system, including memory, the keyboard, the screen, disk drives, line printers, etc.

Hertz (Hz) — a unit of frequency. One Hertz = one cycle per second.

Hexadecimal — a base-16 number system using 16 symbols, 0-9 and A-F. It is used as a convenient "shorthand" way to express *binary** code. For example, 1010 in binary = A in hexadecimal, 11111111 = FF. Hexadecimal is used in constructing patterns for graphics characters in the CALL CHAR subprogram.

Immediate mode — see *Command Mode*.

Increment — a positive or negative value which consistently modifies a *variable**.

Input — (noun) *data** to be placed in computer memory; (verb) the process of transferring data into memory.

Input line — the amount of *data** which can be entered at one time. In TI BASIC, this is 112 characters.

Internal data-format — *data** in the form used directly by the computer. Internal numeric data is 8 *bytes** long plus 1 byte which specifies the length. The length for internal string data is one byte per character in the *string** plus one length-byte.

Integer — a whole number, either positive, negative, or zero.

I/O — Input/Output; usually refers to a device function. I/O is used for communication between the computer and other devices (*e.g.*, keyboard, disk).

*See definition in *Glossary*.

Glossary

Iteration — the technique of repeating a group of program statements; one repetition of such a group. See *Loop*.

Line — see *graphics line*, *input line*, *print line*, or *program line*.

Loop — a group of consecutive program lines which are repeatedly performed, usually a specified number of times.

Mantissa — the base number portion of a number expressed in *scientific notation**. In 3.264E+4, the *mantissa* is 3.264.

Mass storage device — an *accessory device**, such as a cassette recorder or disk drive, which stores programs and/or *data** for later use by the computer. This information is usually recorded in a format readable by the computer, not people.

Memory — see *RAM*, and *ROM*, and *mass storage device*.

Module — see *Command Module*.

Noise — various sounds which can be used to produce interesting sound effects. A *noise*, rather than a tone, is generated by the CALL SOUND *subprogram** when a negative frequency value is specified (−1 through −8).

Null string — a *string** which contains no characters and has zero length.

Number Mode — the mode assumed by the computer when it is automatically generating *program line** numbers for entering or changing statements.

Operator — a symbol used in calculations (numeric operators) or in relationship comparisons (relational operators). The numeric operators are $+,-,*,/,\wedge$. The relational operators are $>,<,=,>=,<=,<>$.

Overflow — the condition which occurs when a rounded value greater than 9.9999999999999E127 or less than −9.9999999999999E127 is entered or computed. When this happens, the value is replaced by the computer's limit, a warning is displayed, and the *program** continues.

Output — (noun) information supplied by the computer; (verb) the process of transferring information from the computer's memory onto a device, such as a screen, line printer, or *mass storage device**.

Parameter — any of a set of values that determine or affect the output of a *statement** or *function**.

Print line — a 28-position line used by the PRINT and DISPLAY statements.

Program — a set of statements which tell the computer how to perform a complete task.

Program line — a line containing a single *statement**. The maximum length of a program line is 112 *characters**.

Prompt — a symbol (>) which marks the beginning of each *command** or *program line** you enter; a symbol or phrase that requests input from the user.

Pseudo-random number — a number produced by a definite set of calculations (algorithm) but which is sufficiently random to be considered as such for some particular purpose. A true random number is obtained entirely by chance.

Radix-100 — a number system based on 100. See "Accuracy Information" for information on number representation.

RAM — random access memory; the main memory where program statements and *data** are temporarily stored during program *execution**. New programs and data can be read in, accessed, and changed in RAM. Data stored in RAM is erased whenever the power is turned off or BASIC is exited.

Record — (noun) a collection of related data elements, such as an individual's payroll information or a student's test scores. A group of similar records, such as a company's payroll records, is called a *file**.

*See definition in *Glossary*.

Glossary

Reserved word — in programming languages, a special word with a predefined meaning. A reserved word must be spelled correctly, appear in the proper order in a *statement** or *command**, and cannot be used as a *variable** name.

ROM — read-only memory; certain instructions for the computer are permanently stored in ROM and can be accessed but cannot be changed. Turning the power off does not erase ROM.

Run Mode — when the computer is *executing** a program, it is in Run Mode. Run Mode is terminated when program execution ends normally or abnormally. You can cause the computer to leave Run Mode by pressing **CLEAR** during program execution (see *Breakpoint**).

Scientific notation — a method of expressing very large or very small numbers by using a base number (*mantissa**) times ten raised to some power (*exponent**). To represent scientific notation in TI BASIC, enter the sign, then the mantissa, the letter E, and the power of ten (preceded by a minus sign if negative). For example, 3.264E4; −2.47E−17.

Scroll — to move the text on the screen so that additional information can be displayed.

Software — various programs which are executed by the computer, including programs built into the computer, *Command Module** programs, and programs entered by the user.

Statement — an instruction preceded by a line number in a program. IN TI BASIC, only one statement is allowed in a *program line**.

String — a series of letters, numbers, and symbols treated as a unit.

Subprogram — a predefined general-purpose procedure accessible to the user through the CALL statement in TI BASIC. Subprograms extend the capability of BASIC and cannot be easily programmed in BASIC.

Subroutine — a program segment which can be used more than once during the *execution** of a program, such as a complex set of calculations or a print routine. In TI BASIC, a subroutine is entered by a GOSUB statement and ends with a RETURN statement.

Subscript — a numeric expression which specifies a particular item in an *array**. In TI BASIC the subscript is written in parentheses immediately following the array name.

Trace — listing the order in which the computer performs program statements. Tracing the line numbers can help you find errors in a program flow.

Underflow — the condition which occurs when the computer generates a numeric value greater than $-1E-128$, less than $1E-128$, and not zero. When an underflow occurs, the value is replaced by zero.

Variable — a name given to a value which may vary during program execution. You can think of a variable as a memory location where values can be replaced by new values during program execution.

Variable-length records — records in a *file** which vary in length depending on the amount of *data** per *record**. Using variable-length records conserves space on a file. Variable-length records can only be accessed sequentially.

---

*See definition in *Glossary*.

Maintenance and Service Information

IN CASE OF DIFFICULTY

In the event that you have difficulty with your computer, the following instructions may help you to analyze the problem. You may be able to correct your computer problem without returning it to a service facility. If the suggested remedies are not successful, contact the Consumer Relations Department by mail or telephone (refer to IF YOU HAVE QUESTIONS OR NEED ASSISTANCE later in this section). Please describe in detail the symptoms of your computer,

If one of the following symptoms appears while operating with the optional peripheral(s) or accessories, remove the device. If the symptom disappears, refer to the manual for the peripheral or accessory in question.

SYMPTOM	*REMEDY*
Console indicator light will not come on when switch is turned on.	■ Check that transformer power cord is plugged into the wall. ■ Ensure that power cord is connected to the rear of the console.
No picture.	■ Check that power is on, and screen controls are set for optimum picture. Ensure that cables are properly connected as specified in the Color Monitor Operating Guide and Warranty.
No sound.	■ See that volume control is turned to proper level. Check connection of cables.
Cassette recorder will not operate when connected to console, but does work properly when not connected.	■ Ensure that cassette is connected to the 9-pin connector on the *rear* of the unit.
Cassette recorder will not Save or Load data properly.	■ See "General Information." ■ Remember that the cassette motor is controlled by the computer. Read the instructions in the "Cassette Interface Cable" section.
Remote Controls will not operate.	■ Ensure that unit is connected to the 9-pin connector on the *left* side of the computer console, and that **ALPHA LOCK** is in the off (up) position. ■ Remember that only certain software is designed for use with the Remote Controls.
BASIC program is cleared by insertion of a Command Module.	■ This is a normal reset procedure designed to protect your color screen.
Stray characters appear or other erratic operation occurs or computer will not respond to keyboard input.	■ Static electricity discharges from the user to the console can alter program data stored in the internal memory. To correct this problem turn the console off and then on.

A Command Module especially designed to verify proper operation of the major functions of your system is available at your retailer. You can also purchase the *Diagnostic* module for use at home.

Maintenance and Service Information

When returning your computer for repair or replacement, return the computer console, power cord, and any Command Modules which were involved when the difficulty occurred. For your protection, the computer should be sent insured; Texas Instruments cannot assume any responsibility for loss or damage to the computer during shipment. It is recommended that the computer be shipped in its original container to minimize the possibility of shipping damage. Otherwise, the computer should be carefully packaged and adequately protected against shock and rough handling. Send shipments to the appropriate Texas Instruments Service Facility listed in the warranty. Please include information on the difficulty experienced with the computer as well as return address information including name, address, city, state and zip code.

If you cannot determine whether the console or the TI Color Monitor/Video Modulator has failed, both units must be returned.

If the computer is in warranty, it will be repaired or replaced under the terms of the Limited Warranty. Out-of-warranty units in need of service will be repaired or replaced with reconditioned units (at TI's option), and service rates in effect at the time of return will be charged. Because our Service Facility serves the entire United States, it is not feasible to hold units while providing service estimates. For advance information concerning service charges, please call our toll-free number listed on the following page.

NOTE: The Color Monitor is too large to be sent via U.S. parcel post (fourth-class mail) but may be sent via first-class mail or by common carrier.

EXCHANGE CENTERS

If your computer requires service, instead of returning the unit to your dealer or to a service facility for repair or replacement, you may elect to exchange the unit for a factory-reconditioned computer of the same model (or equivalent model specified by TI) by bringing it in person to one of the exchange centers which have been established across the United States. A handling fee will be charged by the exchange center for in-warranty exchanges of the computer console and/or TI Color Monitor/Video Modulator. Out-of-warranty exchanges will be charged at the rates in effect at the time of exchange.

To determine if there is an exchange center in your area, look for Texas Instruments Exchange Center in the white pages of your telephone directory, or look under the Calculator and Adding Machine heading in the yellow pages. Please call the exchange center for availability and exchange fee information. Write Consumer Relations for further details and the location of the nearest exchange center.

If you have questions or need assistance

FOR GENERAL INFORMATION

If you have questions concerning computer repair, or peripheral, accessory or software purchase, please call Customer Relations at 800-858-4565 (toll free within the contiguous United States). The operators at these numbers cannot provide technical assistance.

FOR TECHNICAL ASSISTANCE

For technical questions about programming, specific computer applications, etc., you can call 806-741-2663. We regret that this is not a toll-free number, and we cannot accept collect calls.

As an alternative, you can write to:

Consumer Relations
Texas Instruments Incorporated
P.O. Box 53
Lubbock, Texas 79408

Because of the number of suggestions which come to Texas Instruments from many sources containing both new and old ideas, Texas Instruments will consider such suggestions only if they are freely given to Texas Instruments. It is the policy of Texas Instruments to refuse to receive any suggestions in confidence. Therefore, if you wish to share your suggestions with Texas Instruments, or if you wish us to review any BASIC language program which you have developed, please include the following statement in your letter:

"All of the information forwarded herewith is presented to Texas Instruments on a nonconfidential, nonobligatory basis; no relationship, confidential or otherwise, expressed or implied, is established with Texas Instruments by this presentation. Texas Instruments may use, copyright, distribute, publish, reproduce, or dispose of the information in any way without compensation to me."

Index

Index

Index

Index

Three-Month Limited Warranty

THIS TEXAS INSTRUMENTS COMPUTER CONSOLE WARRANTY EXTENDS TO THE ORIGINAL CONSUMER PURCHASER OF THE CONSOLE.

WARRANTY DURATION

This Computer console is warranted for a period of three (3) months from the date of the original purchase by the consumer.

WARRANTY COVERAGE

This Computer console is warranted against defective materials or workmanship. **THIS WARRANTY IS VOID IF THE CONSOLE HAS BEEN DAMAGED BY ACCIDENT, UNREASONABLE USE, NEGLECT, IMPROPER SERVICE OR OTHER CAUSES NOT ARISING OUT OF DEFECTS IN MATERIALS OR WORKMANSHIP.**

WARRANTY DISCLAIMERS

ANY IMPLIED WARRANTIES ARISING OUT OF THIS SALE, INCLUDING BUT NOT LIMITED TO THE IMPLIED WARRANTIES OF MERCHANTABILITY AND FITNESS FOR A PARTICULAR PURPOSE, ARE LIMITED IN DURATION TO THE ABOVE THREE-MONTH PERIOD. TEXAS INSTRUMENTS SHALL NOT BE LIABLE FOR LOSS OF USE OF THE COMPUTER CONSOLE OR OTHER INCIDENTAL OR CONSEQUENTIAL COSTS, EXPENSES, OR DAMAGES INCURRED BY THE CONSUMER OR ANY OTHER USER.

Some states do not allow the exclusion or limitation of implied warranties or consequential damages, so the above limitations or exclusions may not apply to you.

LEGAL REMEDIES

This warranty gives you specific legal rights, and you may also have other rights that vary from state to state.

WARRANTY PERFORMANCE

Please first contact the retailer from whom you purchased the console and determine the exchange policies of the retailer.

During the above three-month warranty period, your TI Computer console will be repaired or replaced with a new or reconditioned console of the same or equivalent model (at TI's option) when the console is returned either in person or by prepaid shipment to a Texas Instruments Service Facility listed below.

Texas Instruments strongly recommends that you insure the console for value, prior to shipment.

The repaired or replacement console will be warranted for three months from date of repair or replacement. Other than the cost of shipping the unit to Texas Instruments or postage, no charge will be made for the repair or replacement of in-warranty consoles.